THE GUINNESS BOOK OF
1952

Kenneth Macksey

GUINNESS SUPERLATIVES LIMITED
2 CECIL COURT, LONDON ROAD, ENFIELD, MIDDLESEX

ACKNOWLEDGEMENTS

All photographs supplied by **POPPERFOTO** except those acknowledged below:

United Press International photos; p. 71 (top), p. 49 (bottom right), p. 87 (right), p. 88 (bottom right), p. 91 (right), Ruston Gas Turbines Ltd., p. 73

Editorial Co-ordinator: Béatrice Frei
Design and layout: David Roberts and Jennifer Sawyer

Published in Great Britain by
Guinness Superlatives Limited, 2 Cecil Court
London Road, Enfield, Middlesex

ISBN 0 900424 40 0

Guinness is a registered trade mark of
Arthur Guinness Son & Co Ltd

Set in 10 pt. Times and
printed and bound in Great Britain by
Redwood Burn Limited, Trowbridge & Esher

OTHER GUINNESS SUPERLATIVES TITLES

Facts and Feats Series:

Air Facts and Feats, *2nd ed.*
John W. R. Taylor, Michael
J. H. Taylor and David Mondey

Rail Facts and Feats, *2nd ed.*
John Marshall

Tank Facts and Feats, *2nd ed.*
Kenneth Macksey

Yachting Facts and Feats
Peter Johnson

Plant Facts and Feats
William G. Duncalf

Structures—Bridges, Towers, Tunnels, Dams . . .
John H. Stephens

Car Facts and Feats, *2nd ed.*
edited by Anthony Harding

Business World
Henry Button and Andrew Lampert

Music Facts and Feats
Bob and Celia Dearling

Animal Facts and Feats, *2nd ed.*
Gerald L. Wood

Guide Series:

Guide to Freshwater Angling
Brian Harris and Paul Boyer

Guide to Mountain Animals
R. P. Bille

Guide to Underwater Life
C. Petron and J. B. Lozet

Guide to Formula 1 Motor Racing
José Rosinski

Guide to Motorcycling, *2nd ed.*
Christian Lacombe

Guide to French Country Cooking
Christian Roland Délu

Guide to Bicycling
Jean Durry

Other titles:

English Furniture 1550–1760
Geoffrey Wills

The Guinness Guide to Feminine Achievements
Joan and Kenneth Macksey

The Guinness Book of Names
Leslie Dunkling

Battle Dress
Frederick Wilkinson

Universal Soldier
edited by Martin Windrow and
Frederick Wilkinson

History of Land Warfare
Kenneth Macksey

History of Sea Warfare
Lt.-Cmdr. Gervis Frere-Cook and
Kenneth Macksey

History of Air Warfare
David Brown, Christopher Shores
and Kenneth Macksey

The Guinness Book of Answers
edited by Norris D. McWhirter

The Guinness Book of Records, *23rd ed.*
edited by Norris D. McWhirter

CONTENTS

INTRODUCTION

At the advent of the year 1952, the world presented a jumbled picture of hope mixed with impending doom set in a framework of gloom and despondency. A quarter of a century later, it is possible to look back and scrape the memory while asking if things have changed all that much in the interim. It is also enjoyable to titillate the nostalgia, by wondering if events really were as bad as they sometimes looked at the time. There was then a world recession, rapidly rising prices, industrial strife and material shortages, all adding up to, or caused by, a sharp outbreak of inflation. Fear lay deeply rooted in people's minds even though the World War had ended in 1945, but it was a fear based on a sense of fundamental insecurity, fermented by a volatile political situation, which was presented by the news media as belonging to a world standing close to the brink of total destruction from an atomic holocaust. Mistrust abounded, and was stimulated by intensive propaganda. In those places where there was an armed truce in the Cold War, the Russians let it be known they feared the West's intentions, while the countries of the West took measures to protect themselves against what they judged to be Russia's ambitions of conquest. Precautions against the Communist infiltration of Western Society ran amok, notably in the USA where the McCarthy witch hunt was gathering momentum. So the cynic may ask, 25 years later, have things changed so very much?

Somehow life went on and, to those who had been most closely affected by the war years, it seemed actually to be improving in quality. The scars of war were slowly being healed as new buildings rose above the ruins. The luxuries some people craved were beginning to fill the shop windows and, at a price, foreign travel was becoming possible again on a fairly large scale, especially for the affluent Americans. In many more communities people were beginning to enjoy themselves, to relax again. With a few clear-cut reservations, they began to behave in the hope that tomorrow might come—even if the Bomb did vaguely seem to threaten the very existence of the world—and to abandon the feverish wartime philosophy of 'tomorrow we die'.

SECTION 1
THE HEADLINES

The Flying Enterprise

The New Year opened with the news media dominated by a gripping saga of the sea in the most heroic mould. On 26 December 1951, the cargo of the US registered 6711 ton SS *Flying Enterprise* had shifted in heavy seas while 300 miles from England. The ship had listed to 30° and her hull split, but although much water had been shipped she was still afloat when, on 31 December, rescue ships managed to save the ten passengers and 38 members of the crew of 40. One, however, was lost and the Captain, **Henrik Carlson,** remained on board in the belief that the ship might be towed to port and its cargo of pig iron, antiques, pottery and coffee (insured in all at $1 750 000) saved. In remaining aboard, Carlson tried to ensure that his vessel would remain his company's property instead of falling into the hands of the successful salvage agents. On 3 January the British salvage tug *Turmoil* arrived and next day, after attempts to fix a line had failed, its mate,

The Flying Enterprise

Kenneth Dancy, leapt aboard to join the captain on the ship whose list was now 60°. On the 5th a line was secured and a tow, at 3 knots, begun in improving weather. But when, on the 8th, they were only 50 miles from Falmouth a fresh storm blew up, the line broke and attempts to resecure it failed.

A Crisis in Sterling

Winston Churchill with (left) *R A Butler and* (right) *Hugh Gaitskill*

A crisis in sterling related to the strength of the US dollar plagued the Conservative Government, under **Winston Churchill,** and with it inflation (at about 5% for food after a reduction in subsidies) that was described by **L S Amery** as being in 'full canter and . . . might at any moment break into a headlong gallop'. Churchill himself arrived in the USA on the *Queen Mary* for talks with **President Harry Truman,** at which it was agreed that the USA would sell Britain one million tons of steel and purchase, in return, 20 000 tons of tin, 22 300 tons of

aluminium and 25 000 tons of rubber in order, mainly, to implement their respective enormous rearmament programmes. Back in England **R A Butler**, the Chancellor of the Exchequer, grappled with a record deficit of £334 million in the last quarter of 1951 by the time honoured expedients of reducing Government expenditure, cutting imports by £150 million and borrowing abroad. On 29 January the nation was told that fewer goods were to be manufactured for the home market, hire purchase restrictions were to be stiffened, the Civil Service was to be reduced and foreign travel, for other than urgent business reasons, made virtually impossible. On 1 January Sterling was regulated at about $2.80 (25 years later it was less than $2 in a free market) and the **rationing of food** was still in being 6½ years after the end of the war. Nevertheless, the ensuing year was to see a gradual relaxation or removal of Government controls over commodities and services: licensing of food retailers was abolished by the Ministry of Food in October, tea came off ration in October too, and the bulk purchase of such items as cocoa and fertilizer had ended by the end of the year, in accordance with Conservative Party policy announced before the previous election in October 1951.

Rioting in Egypt

The violence which had brought death and destruction to Egypt in 1951 continued. Ambushes of British troops were met with tough retaliation by the British with artillery and tanks against terrorists and rebellious police. Ten days after **King Farouk's** Queen had given birth to a

son and heir, the most serious rioting of all broke out on 26 January in the centre of Cairo. British, French and American commercial buildings, the famous Shepheards Hotel and the British Turf Club were burnt. In compensation the Egyptian Government later offered £5 million. Egyptian Governments were to come and go for the next six months against a backcloth of martial law and constantly changing personalities. However, on 6 February the attention of everybody in Britain and, for that matter, the greater part of the civilised world, turned towards London when there came the shock announcement of the death, in his sleep, of **King George VI**.

Death of a King

and Accession of a Queen

The King had been ailing for many years and died from lung cancer. On 31 January he had made his last public appearance, seeing off to Kenya Princess Elizabeth and the Duke of Edinburgh. From an overnight stay in the Tree Top Hotel near Nyeri they flew home immediately as the nation went into ten days' mourning. On 8 February the new Sovereign was proclaimed **Queen Elizabeth II**, and Churchill made a memorable speech over the radio in which he referred to a King who had walked with death as if death were an acquaintance he did not fear. The

The last picture of King George VI

Searching Egyptians for arms

Funeral cortège at Windsor

King's body lay in State at Westminster Hall throughout the 12th, 13th and 14th while over 300 000 people filed past in respect. The funeral took place on the 15th, a grey, cold day made solemn by the silence of the crowds lining the route of the procession from Westminster to Paddington railway terminus, the boom of the guns and the slow, measured tones of several military bands echoing and re-echoing through the streets. From Windsor station the coffin was taken to St George's Chapel and there laid to rest.

To a nation tired of the terror of war, the gloom of financial stringency and the oft-proclaimed **'Austerity'**, the proclamation of a Queen with such an evocative name acted as a stimulant—a theme to which the propagandist quickly bent their skill in promoting. A subject for much comment was attributable to a remark once made by the Queen's father that she was 'a poor lonely girl' who would be lonely all her life. But her intense interest in horses certainly reflected an inherent preoccupation among her subjects. It was noticed that she spent more time at Ascot than her father, was the first monarch to visit Goodwood for 20 years and broke her holiday in Scotland in order to watch the St Leger and became extremely excited during the closing stages of any race. Yet on the great occasions of State she performed her duties with a mature dignity that was entirely in keeping with her promise to devote her whole life to her people.

Queen Elizabeth II with (left to right) *The Hon D S Senanayake (Ceylon), Sir Godfrey Huggins (Southern Rhodesia), Rt Hon S G Holland (New Zealand), Sir Winston Churchill, Rt Hon Menzies (Australia), Rt Hon L S St Laurent (Canada), The Hon N C Havenga (South Africa), The Hon Khwaja Nazimuddin (Pakistan) and Mr C D Deshmukw (India)*

Templer goes to Malaya

Throughout the year attention became focused repeatedly upon events in the Far East. **In Malaya the State of Emergency** brought about by Communist insurrection in 1948 continued, with the end not even in sight. Yet a turning point, unrecognised at the time, was reached with the arrival on 7 February of **General Sir Gerald Templer** as the new High Commissioner, merging in him the civil and military functions of government in a situation which demanded a political solution as an essential basis of the one by force. Victories in local elections by the **United Malays National Organisation** in February, when 70% of the registered voters went to the poll, ran parallel with the formation of a Malayan Federation Regiment which was to admit members of all races; the introduction in July of compulsory service for all able-bodied Malayans

General Templer punishes villagers

in the defence forces; and a strict tightening up of security measures, allied with firm, punitive action against those who helped the terrorists. On 25 August, for example, the village of **Permatang Tinggi** was destroyed and its 70 inhabitants sent to detention for failure to give information about the murder of a Chinese official. On the same day the Indian Government asked the British to stop recruiting Gurkha soldiers on Indian territory—the Gurkhas being a main stay of the British military in Malaya. However, the year saw a gradual decline in the number of people killed by terrorism, an increase in the number of terrorists eliminated and a steady rise in confidence throughout the country.

War in Korea

The war in Korea went on with random outbursts of bitter fighting along the entrenched front that had been established in 1951 and to the accompaniment of the prolonged **armistice negotiations already taking place at Panmunjong**. On 9 January the Communists accepted a number of United Nations conditions, and on 17 February the United Nations agreed to a Communist proposal to hold a conference in connection with Korean problems after the armistice. In October the conference broke down. A major bone of contention was the large number of prisoners held by each side, some 121 000 Communists and 12 700 United Nations of whom 945 were British, and 3597 American. While most of the UN wished for repatriation, far fewer among the Communists had any such desire. Anxious to gain a political advantage, Communist agents were infiltrated among Korean internees and Northern prisoners of war in various camps throughout the South to stimulate riots, sometimes by killing those prisoners who resisted their proposals. On 18 February a riot took place among 1500 of the 5000 civilian internees on Koje Island, in which one US soldier, and 69 internees were killed. More riots followed elsewhere, each bringing its toll of dead and wounded.

North Korean prisoners of war rioting

Matters came to a head on 7 May when the Koje prisoners lured the prison commandant, **Brigadier-General Francis Dodd**, into their own hands and released him only after concessions and receipt of a 'ransom note' which they immediately used as a propaganda device to demonstrate their 'maltreatment'. Refuting the note, once Dodd had been released, the new commandant sent in 1000 paratroops with tanks to smash the revolt (at a cost in dead of one paratrooper and 38 prisoners) and split the prisoners up into smaller compounds. Further disturbances continued throughout the year though these never got out of control again.

Austerity and the first Butler Budget

The first Budget under the new British Conservative Government was introduced by R A Butler on 11 March 'to restore confidence in the pound'. Food subsidies were lowered, thus adding 1s 6d (7½p) per head per week to the family bill; petrol 7½d (3p) per gallon added, an excess profits tax of 30% above 1947–9 levied, and Bank Rate put up from 2½% to 4%. At the same time relief was given on Income Tax allowances, pensions were increased, and Family Allowance raised from 5s (25p) to 8s (40p) per week per child, and the Utility Goods scheme abolished. To everyone's surprise this 'looked' like a rejection of 'Austerity', and so the Budget was greeted with relief by many people and as the signal for the **National Union of Mine Workers** (stimulated by **Hugh Gaitskill**, the leader of the Labour Opposition) to announce that since it was 'a direct attack on the living standards of working people', a general rise in wages was demanded. Yet on 6 April Mr Butler announced that 'Austerity' might still be needed even though the dollar deficit, which had been $299 million in January, was only $71 million in March. And in August the Trades Union Congress supported the Conservative Government in its campaign against general wage increase, taking the line that a rise in the price of goods would cut exports. But in the USA, for example, where receipts from tax rose to an estimated $62 800 million in 1952 compared with $48 143 million in 1951, the Cost of Living remained virtually static in an economy that was strong and healthy.

The Apartheid battle

The constitutional struggle in South Africa over what is now more generally known as the policy of **Apartheid** but which, on its introduction in 1951, had been the Separate Representation of Voters Act that removed the Cape Coloured electors from the common voters role, created a fierce debate which, in different forms, is easily re-generated 25 years later. On 20 March 1952 the Supreme Court ruled that the Act was invalid because it had not been passed by joint session of both Houses. In response the Prime Minister, **Dr Daniel Malan**, declared that the situation was 'intolerable' and he proceeded to introduce a Bill setting up a 'High Court of Parliament', to override the Appellate Division in matters concerning Parliament. Tension mounted, the **Torch Commandos** and Opposition parties joined forces to resist the Bill, but it was passed on 29 May. In August the new **High Court of Parliament** restored the Separate Voters Act. On 29 August, however, the Cape Bench ruled that the High Court of Parliament itself was invalid, a decision that was later supported by five appeal judges at Bloemfontein. So Dr Malan was compelled to accept defeat, for the time being, and conceed that, in the next General Election, the coloured voters would vote on the common roll. In parallel with the constitutional debate, however, there arose a movement pledged to resist Apartheid by means of selected civil disobedience. But while there was only a smattering of actual violence as the result of law breaking, (mostly towards the end of the year) the clenched fist salute by coloured people in defiance of the White rulers was more and more to be seen. Government reaction to disobedience declared itself in a recurrent resort to the Suppres-

Dr Malan

sion of Communism Act on the grounds, with some justification, that Communists were the principal agents behind the troubles.

The Web of Treaties

This was, indeed, a year in which the headlines were frequently starred by major diplomatic events, one in which the Western Powers endeavoured through treaties to consolidate a collective front against Communism and the ever more strongly militant nationalist movements. In the Far East the potential of the Chinese threat was most noticeable by their presence on the North Korean side. At the end of April the **Peace Treaty between Japan and the USA** and 48 other past enemies took force. Communist China was not included and Soviet Russia, Poland and Czechoslovakia refused to sign—a state of affairs which exists 25 years later in respect of the latter three. Since Japan stood without defence forces of her own, the responsibility for defence continued to rest upon the USA which received money and land from the Japanese for this purpose—set against substantial US financial aid in other sectors. On the same date the mutual defence of 1951 between the USA, Australia and New Zealand (the **ANZUS Pact**) also came into effect, having been ratified by the USA in March. In Europe the **North Atlantic Treaty Organisation** continued in its efforts to strengthen its defences by vast injections of wealth, mostly originating from the USA. On 2 April **General Dwight Eisenhower** made his first and last report as its Supreme Commander, and concluded that, although the future looked bright, much needed to be done. In particular, he cited the need for greater collaboration between the European Nations, through such projects as the

Signing the Anzus Pact

Schuman Plan—named after Robert Schuman—(see below) and the creation of a **European Army**. At the same time he asked to be relieved of his command in order to take part in the forthcoming Presidential election campaign (see below).

European unification was a dominant issue if only because an oft-quoted need seemed suddenly to some, under the Soviet Russian threat, to have become essential. At the same time strong fears were expressed in the realisation that the intention of such a scheme was the **reincarnation of German military power**—with all that implied through memories of the past.

Robert Schuman and party

The first Jet Airliner Service

The pioneering of jet propelled aircraft, both in the military and civil field, found Britain very much in the lead, particularly with regard to civil types. Controversy raged over the commercial practicalities of operating airliners such as the turbo-propeller powered **Vickers Viscount**, or pure jet versions such as the **DH Comet**. The Viscount had been the first of its type into service in 1950 and was already a worldwide success, popular with passengers for its speed and quiet smoothness of flight, and with operators for its reliability and economical performance. It was argued that the pure jet airliner could not hope to compete with the turbo-prop despite its higher speed and even greater passenger appeal. Matters were put to the test as the first jet airline service in the world was inaugurated when a British Overseas Airways Comet flew from London to Johannesburg on 2 May, carrying 36 passengers the 6724 miles in 23 hours 34 minutes, with stops at Rome, Beirut, Khartoum, Entebbe and Livingstone. Orders began to pour in for both the Viscount and the Comet; one, much prized, was that from Pan-American World Airlines in October for three of the projected Comet III, when ready—the hesitant American aircraft industry having staked on conventional engines for its airliners and thereby fallen ten years behind in technology. Britain's aircraft industry rode the crest of a wave as the fruits of post-war design activity began to appear—the 95 seater **Bristol Britannia**, the 140 ton **Saunders Roe Princess** flying boat with its ten turbo-prop engines, the first delta winged bomber in the world, (the four jet **Avro Vulcan**) and many more, each hitting the headlines in turn.

Persian Oil and Dr Musaddiq

The nationalisation of British oil interests in Persia, which had taken place in 1951 under the leadership of the Persian Prime Minister, **Dr Mohammed Musaddiq**, continued to fascinate the world; this was partly because of the principles involved and the intricacies of the legal battle being waged by Britain to prevent Persian oil being sold on the world market, and, as much as anything else, for the dramatic and, at times, unpredictable performance of Musaddiq himself. While definitive action in the International Court of Justice was pending, the International Bank offered to act as trustee of the oilfield, but admitted failure in March 1952. In the meantime Persia's inability to sell her oil caused a serious revenue shortage

The D H Comet at Khartoum

at a time when the Communist Tudeh Party was provoking general unrest and assailing the position of the Shah. Musaddiq was forever seeking the limelight, while at the same time trying to steer a neutral course with the Russians and their Communist collaborators and tackling the British with fiery intransigence. It was natural that the British news media should heap calumny upon their country's tormentor and have a field day at the expense of a man whose patriotism was undeniable, but whose instability and habit of fainting when under stress laid him open to ridicule. In June, against a background of serious unrest in Persia, Dr Musaddiq in person pleaded his country's case against Britain before the International Court at the Hague and persuaded them to rule, on 22 July, in Persia's favour, saying they had no jurisdiction in the case. Early in July, however, Musaddiq had been overthrown as Prime Minister. Later reinstated by the Majlis (though with so little enthusiasm that he refused to serve unless granted dictatorial powers), he was replaced by a new Prime Minister on 17 July and then brought back to power once again on the 22nd after Tudeh led riots, egged on by himself, had threatened civil war. The remainder of the year in Persia passed to the accompaniment of a rising crescendo of Musaddiq inspired crises—the eventual grant of dictatorial powers to Musaddiq; a round of fluctuating negotiations, with the USA, Russian and Indian Governments left in constant uncertainty; a progressive undermining of the Shah's authority; the pursuit of the vendetta against the British leading to the breaking of diplomatic relations on 22 October; and the steady decline of Persian solvency when oil revenue dried up under threat of British legal action such as that already taken in the case of oil shipped in the tanker *Rose Marie*.

Dr Musaddiq

European Unity

The mounting impetus of the movement towards **closer unity among European nations** reached something of a climax in the spring and summer. In the east the Soviet Russian influence persisted with its own unyielding mandatory kind of hold upon the subject nations, but in the West there was keen public debate. Marshall Aid was due to expire at the end of June and was to be replaced by a Mutual Security Programme which enabled the USA to continue assistance to her allies in both the military and economic spheres. However, the USA, which was budgeting for foreign aid grants of $3646 millions for Europe, desired a considerably greater European effort in return. In 1951 a treaty establishing the European Coal and Steel Community (ECSC) by which France, West Germany, Holland, Belgium, Luxembourg and Italy agreed to a common market for those two products, had been signed and was due for implementation in July 1952. **This, the Schuman Plan, laid the foundation of today's Common Market.** Fresh life to the moribund, consultative **Council of Europe** was given by **Mr Anthony Eden** in March, when he suggested ways of associating the Council with the ECSC. Negotiations then proceeded to create a **European Defence Community** (EDC) of the signatories of the ECSC, and this was accepted on 30 May, just three days after the Treaty for the Defence Pact was signed. The EDC aimed at the creation of a **European Army,** with uniform conscription and standardisation of equipment among its clauses, along with control of the more 'perilous' weapons, such as the atomic and bacteriological type. Essentially, German armed forces were to be raised again and this, in due course, was to lead to the rejection of the Treaty by the French in 1954. Nevertheless, long strides forward were being made, with British proposals for links with the ECSC finding willing acceptance in September, the same month in which it was agreed to set up a **European Court of Justice.** A man who stood at the pinnacle of European affairs was **M Jean Monnet** (France) who, as President of the High Authority of the ECSC, said, 'All these institutions can be changed and improved by experience. What will not be changed is their supra-national and—let us say it—federal character.'

Anthony Eden

Jean Monnet

Harry Truman

The first Nuclear Ship

On 14 June President Truman laid the keel of what would be the USS submarine *Nautilus*—**the world's first nuclear powered vessel.** In so doing he inaugurated a revolution in naval warfare, for this new ship was to be not so remarkable in so much as she would have an underwater speed in excess of 20 knots, but because her power plant would enable her to cruise for just so long as air supplies and provisions would allow—for 50 000 miles without refuelling or maintenance if necessary. Already the power plant, a uranium-fuelled thermal reactor, was advanced in development, and in January it had been announced that work was to begin on a surface vessel, a nuclear powered aircraft carrier. Much more attention was now being focused on the peaceful as well as the warlike uses of nuclear energy, and the demand for crucial materials

was leaping ahead. A **'Uranium Rush'** began with extensive searches by geologists everywhere and the announcement by Canada on 4 August of large areas in Saskatchewan open for 'staking'. Meanwhile Britain produced her first plutonium from pitch blend obtained from the Belgian Congo.

Laying the keel of USS Nautilus

Air Warfare over Korea

While the war on land in Korea stood in stalemate, awaiting the outcome of the Armistice negotiations, aircraft were always aloft in search of information and attempting, on the United Nation's part, to reduce if not cripple the North Korean war effort. Since 1950 jet had fought jet in 'Mig Alley' over the Yalu River, the frontier zone between Korea and Manchuria. Beyond this the United Nations were forbidden to bomb, though, to the south of it, anything of economic or military value was attacked whenever possible. On 23 June a series of heavy raids involving 500 aircraft were initiated against hydro-electric power stations along the Yalu on its southern bank. A debate in the House of Commons made it clear that members were annoyed at not being previously consulted by the Americans, though eventually they seemed fairly satisfied that bombs had not fallen across the frontier. The raids went on and the following four months alone were to see 42 000 tons of bombs and 200 000 gallons of flaming napalm, in addition to rockets, poured on the North Koreans. As a result it was claimed that North Korean war capacity had been reduced to 25%

Bombing of Pyongyang by US aircraft

and its people's morale had suffered. However, Chinese supplies and reinforcements continued to cross from Manchuria and the front remained stable despite heavy Chinese land offensives in October.

Coups in the Middle East

Several changes in the Egyptian Governments of King Farouk marked the first six months of a year which saw no improvement of relations between the British and Egyptians. Guerilla warfare was sporadic but unending. All went into the melting pot on 23 July, however, when a military *coup d'état* suddenly swept **General Mohammed Neguib** to power in Cairo. Behind the *coup* stood a small group of Army officers who for years had been dissatisfied with the way the country and the forces were being run and, particularly, with certain arms scandals and corruption. The planning genius behind them was an unknown and, for some time, obscure Colonel by the name of **Gemal Nasser**. Three days' inept manoeuvring by the King merely exhausted the officers' patience and on the 26th he was compelled to abdicate and leave the country for ever. Egypt was in turmoil for several months while the Army tightened its grip, abolished ancient titles and the Monarchy, suspended the political parties, introduced land reforms, purged their own ranks and severely put down rioting which broke out in August near Alexandria.

British artillery in Korea

King Talal unfit to rule because of chronic schizophrenia and replace him by his 17 year old son, **Hussein**. There were few, in those days, who envied his future or prospects for survival. Still a minor, and plunged into an explosive environment, Hussein had witnessed his grandfather's assassination in 1951, and for nearly a year was to be subject to a regency council.

King Hussein dancing at the Dorchester

Mohammed Neguib

For the time being pressure came off the British since Neguib had to concentrate on internal politics and, not least, a solution of financial strains and the feeding of a population who looked for quick benefits from a Revolutionary regime. The British, too, had their preoccupations elsewhere in the region, for on 11 August both Houses of the Jordanian Parliament felt the need to pronounce

Lynmouth Flooded

The year was to undergo its full share of calamities (mentioned, too, in Section 8) but some (not necessarily the greatest by any means) caught the public's imagination more than others. The deluge at Lynmouth on 16 August was a case in point. After 9 inches of rain had fallen on Exmoor in 24 hours (5 inches in 5 hours at one period) and turned streams into torrents, the West Lyn River diverted from its course and passed through the town's main street, causing damage up to about £3 million by sweeping away 17 bridges, destroying 33 houses and seriously damaging 42 others, taking 95 cars (some into the sea) and killing 31 people. Rated the greatest natural disaster of the century in Great Britain, the widespread publicity it attracted brought a vast response. The Relief Fund gathered in about £300 000 in cash by the end of the month in addition to 180 000 parcels, the majority of which remained unopened. Yet in terms of human suffering, death and destruction the Lynmouth disaster was small compared with, for example, the **tornado which had struck the USA** in March, causing over 236 deaths and millions of dollars damage with countless homeless, and the famine which was likely to ensue from the **locust plague** then ravaging parts of the **Middle East and India**.

The Mau Mau Rebellion

Since the war the Colony of Kenya had benefited by substantial investment by European, mainly British, settlers. Participation by the indigenous peoples was very limited. Such resentment as existed dwelt mainly among the big Kikuyu tribe, some of whose members began a systematic attack upon law and order early in the year. Their own secret society, the **Mau Mau**, initiated its members at bestial oath-taking ceremonies (which were as abhorrent to many Kenyans as to Europeans), and recruited a large following sworn to the elimination of foreign influence in government and religion with a view to taking control of the country into their own hands. A campaign of murder and terror was aimed primarily at those Africans—mainly Kikuyu—who withstood the Mau Mau and it obtained such a hold upon those threatened that evidence was almost impossible to obtain in criminal cases. A £2500 fine, imposed upon five Kikuyu villages in April over hut-burning, did little good at a time

Jomo Kenyatta

when the outside world hardly realised what was impending. It was attacks upon a few Europeans which brought the subject to wider attention, including the attempted assassination of some Roman Catholic missionaries in September. On 20 October a State of Emergency was declared, and arrangements made to reinforce the police by British troops, local reserves and a Home Guard. Next day **Jomo Kenyatta**, the President of the Kenya African Union since 1947, was arrested along with a number of other militant Kikuyu and put on trial in November for his activities in connection with the Mau Mau. But it was to be another seven years before the Mau Mau was finally eliminated, years in which the Kikuyu tribe, more than any other, was to suffer for its independence of intention, and the horrifying methods employed by the Mau Mau cult.

Mau Mau terrorists

The Olympic Games

Being a Leap Year, 1952 was also the time for the dominating sporting event, another round of **Olympic Games**—beginning with the VIth Winter Games at Oslo in February with 30 nations taking part. It is probably true to say that it was the enthusiasm of the Norwegians which made this the first occasion on which the winter games achieved popular appeal. Crowds were enormous (130 000 at times) as a great many people arrived from overseas to witness the events; the Norwegians themselves dominated by taking seven Gold and nine other medals with **Hjalmar Anderson** winning the 1500, 5000 and 10 000 metres speed skating events. For Britain there was one Gold—that won by **Jeanette Altwegg** in the Women's Figure Skating. The main summer events—the XVth Games—were held in July at Helsinki; the flame was lit on the 19th by the great Finnish long-distance runner, **Paavo Nurmi**. Prior to this **Avery Brundage** of the USA was elected as President of the International Committee, a post he was to hold until 1972. After the flame was lit, a woman clothed in white ran towards the rostrum with the intention of delivering an unofficial speech, but was intercepted by those more fleet of foot. The Games themselves, with nearly 6000 competitors from 69 nations, were notable not so much for the high performances achieved or the expected preponderance of medals won by the USA and the USSR, as for the 16 Gold, 10 Silver and 16 Bronze medals taken home by Hungary. Probably the most celebrated name competing was that of the Czechoslovakian **Zatopek family**: the husband, Emil, took the 5000 metres, 10 000 metres and the marathon while his wife, Dana, won Gold in the women's javelin. For Britain the Games were a dismal experience, her only Gold medal coming at the very last moment by the horsemen taking the team event in the Prix des Nations. Overall about 200 Olympic and World Records were broken including seven of the latter.

The Zatopek family

Great Britain joins the Atomic Bomb Club

Although Britain had played a crucial part in making the original US manufactured atomic bomb possible, Russia had been the next nation to possess this weapon, and it was not until October 1952 that Britain tested her own. The test took place at the Monte Bello Islands, off Western Australia, on 2 October, when a device stowed in the 1370 ton frigate HMS *Plym* was detonated, totally vaporising the ship while throwing up the familiar mushroom shaped cloud. Commenting on the achievement in the House of Commons and congratulating the members of the previous Labour Government who had made this possible, Churchill remarked that 'as an old

Left: *Britain's A-Bomb and* right: *the USA's H-Bomb*

parliamentarian I was rather astonished that something well over £100 million could be disbursed without Parliament being made aware of it.' However, in the USA they were concocting something yet more gigantic—the world's **first Hydrogen Bomb**—and this they exploded at Eniwetok on 1 November with truly stunning results. For in due course (though not at the time) it came to be known that this device generated the equivalent of 5 to 7 million tons of TNT explosive (or 5 to 7 megatons as it came to be

known) and it had dug a hole one mile wide and 175 ft deep totally removing the island upon which it had stood. Revolutionary to the practice of diplomacy and war-making though the first atomic bomb had been in 1945, the advent of this new super-weapon threw every calculation to the winds. So overwhelming were the effects of this, the so-called 'Ultimate Deterrent', that minds boggled at the prospect of any sort of nuclear war in the future. A whole new train of thoughts and reactions was given impetus in the political field.

Eisenhower elected as President of the USA

On 2 January after a long period of speculation, **Dwight Eisenhower** had announced that, if asked, he would stand

as the Republican candidate, and on 11 July he was chosen by the party convention at the first vote. A few days later the Democrats chose **Adlai Stevenson,** a rather unwilling candidate who, for all his superior intellectual

Eisenhower and Nixon electioneering

ability, lacked the popular appeal of his rival. The campaign that followed was remarkable in that it was the first in which television played an important role by bringing the contenders to closer public attention.

Adlai Stevenson

Eisenhower made it one of his election pledges that he would end the war in Korea. Carrying out the traditional whistle stop tour, he travelled 50 000 miles and made over 200 speeches. But there came a bit of a hiccup in the closing stages of his campaign when his running partner for Vice-President, one **Richard Nixon**, was abruptly accused

by his opponents of being the beneficiary from a large political fund. On television and radio Nixon defended his use of the money for political purposes and accused his adversaries of malpractice. The Republican party and Eisenhower backed him up, though there were voices which suggested that Eisenhower's anti-corruption campaign looked a little thin just then. More accusations from both sides followed, with Eisenhower and Stevenson feeling compelled to reveal details of their income tax returns over the previous ten years—an example which Mr Nixon decided not to emulate. The result of the election was a decisive victory for Eisenhower with 39 to 9 States voting in his favour and a total of 33 927 549 votes to Stevenson's 27 311 316. The Republicans also gained control of both Houses, though with slim majorities. A few days later Eisenhower announced his Cabinet of whom **John Foster Dulles,** as Secretary of State, was to become the most celebrated by his style of personal diplomacy and 'an infinite capacity for taking planes'.

War in Indo-China

While Eisenhower was quick to visit Korea to see things for himself prior to taking up the reins of office in January 1953, a war that was every bit as destructive continued in **French Indo China** against the Communist inspired **Viet Minh**. The death of the French Commander-in-Chief, **Marshal Lattre de Tassigny**, in January (see Section 9) left a gap that could not adequately be filled, particularly while the French Government was for ever in turmoil (see below). The heavy fighting in specific areas, such as the Red River Delta in the approaches to Hanoi, was

Action in Indo-China

undertaken against a widespread pattern of guerilla warfare in which the insurgent forces coerced the populace to work in their favour. The French, although they had committed about one third of their army to the struggle, were barely holding their own. Both the USA and Russia entered more deeply into the act by supplying arms and materials, each side appreciating that the fate of something more than Indo-China itself was at stake. A Viet Minh offensive that began in October made steady headway despite French counter-attacks, and the end of the year found them in retreat in every place where the pressure was on.

The frequently changing French Governments

A source of constant wonder to the British as well as consternation to those who had France's well-being at heart, were the repeated changes in Government that took place in that country throughout the year. Budgetary problems and lost votes of confidence in Assemblies, where the parties were fragmented and unstable, led three Prime Ministers to come and go—**M Pinay** being the last to resign on 23 December, leaving France without a Government at the New Year. Yet there was continuity of a sort running parallel with the fluctuations. **Robert Schuman** had been Foreign Secretary since 1948, surviving all the changes, and **Charles de Gaulle** remained true to himself and those who backed Gaullism by forming a parliamentary group of his own in July.

At the end of the year

While **M René Mayer** tried to form a new Government in France, Winston Churchill set sail once more for Jamaica via the USA; skirmishing went on across the world's many battlefronts; the Communists accused the US of shelling the armistice site at Panmunjon; and the South Africans beat Australia in the second Test Match at Melbourne. Yet the British newspapers in their new year valedictory messages did not sound unduly pessimistic about the future for it seemed that, at last, Austerity was on the way out in company with the old year.

Seeing the old year out in Piccadilly

SECTION 2

THE EVERYDAY SCENE

The Weather

That mainstay topic of conversation, the weather, was well stimulated by outrages of its performance in 1952 and they were quite sufficiently unpleasant to satisfy the conclusions of those who blamed its worst lapses on atomic tests. In Britain and the rest of Europe remarkable extremes of perfidy were experienced; in America and the Far East there occured the customary number of gigantic calamities (described in Section 8).

The winter in Britain was cold, with 1°F registered at **Logie Coldstone** in Scotland on 30 January. Heavy snow fell in southern England at the end of March, and in **Marseilles** it actually snowed on 4 April. By the middle of April, however, the temperature had recovered to register as much as 77°F in **Berlin** on the 12th, in **London** it was the warmest May since 1848 and **New York** had its hottest July since 1871—an average 87.1°F. Throughout England a generally warm and dry summer ensued—until August, when the holiday-makers were out in force. Then, on 6 August, as a foretaste of what was to come, no less than 3.25 inches of rain fell in 2 hours at **Boreham Wood, Herts.,** in a day in which 4.83 inches fell locally with resultant flooding. Exceeding this by far was the 9 inches that fell on one part of Exmoor which caused the **Lynmouth flood disaster** (see Sections 1 and 8). In France rain storms which swept the Riviera on 19 August, came just in time to extinguish the forest fires which had begun on the 18th in conditions of heavy drought. Extremes of temperature were also the order of the day in the following month, with the coldest September day in Oxfordshire since 1811 that heralded four months of persistent cold lasting until the end of the year, a period punctuated by four days of almost continuous fog (or smog) of the most injurious kind in the first week of December.

January in London

Relatively few people, compared with 1976, travelled far to take part in skiing in those days, and mostly they left Britain by sea and rail. In the winter months of 1952, however, ample snow fell in the first few months (in places the heaviest for a century) and the last quarter of the year brought the first snow early in September in the Dolomites which spread rapidly with bitter cold in attendance.

July in Blackpool

The Population

Of crucial importance to the pattern of everyday life was population density and its steady growth, estimated on a world-wide basis, at about 2% per annum; the rise was due very largely to the reduction of the death rate. **National growth rates** varied considerably, of course, depending upon local conditions. In Europe it was about 5%, in Asia 3% and in North America 1.75%. Inevitably, in terms of general standards of living, this was beginning to put a strain on the world's capacity to support so many people. While the outstandingly high standards of consumption in the USA concealed from the American people the approaching gravity of the situation, those who lived in places such as China and India, where frequent famines were a background to the way of life, took another view. As yet the movement towards strict birth control in China and India was severely hampered by a general unwillingness to recognise that birth control was a key to raising living standards. Nonetheless, the world's surface was estimated in 1952 to carry 2400 million people at a density, excluding Antarctica, of 41.2 per square mile with **the Saar holding the record for the most highly populated country** at 1155 persons per square mile.

Employment

The number of people engaged in different kinds of employment varied substantially. Statistics for Britain and the USA with their mixed economies were as follows in mid-year:

	Britain (000)	USA (000)
Agriculture and Fishing	1142	10 000
Civil Government Service	1365	6585
Mining and Quarrying	873	862
Public Utilities	368	4170
Transport and Communications	1762	
Manufacturing	8571	15 609
Building etc	1447	2661
Distributive Trades	2628	9787
Professional and Financial Service	3985	6817
Military Service	872	3629
Unemployment	489	1578

The fast rising level of prices in 1951 naturally had its effect on **wage demands** in 1952 with the resultant threat or implementation of **strike action**. By and large there was little serious disruption in Britain where disputes were mostly local and settled by arbitration or negotiation. The miners set an example and moved towards higher production in April by voting about 5 to 1 to recommence Saturday working. Nevertheless, the miners accounted for the highest number of lost working days throughout the year with the motor industry coming second. An unofficial strike of 7790 men at **Briggs Motor Bodies, Dagenham**, from 12 June until 15 July, over a 9d (4p) per hour pay claim, severely affected production at **Ford Motors**.

In the USA there was a grim struggle between the Administration and labour and a three fold rise in cases of industrial action, compared with 1951, as workers fought to obtain pay rises and the employers attempted to increase the price of their products against **President Truman's** wishes. His biggest clash came with the **United Steelworkers** who called a 53 day strike from 3 June to 24 July involving 600 000 men. Already, however, there had been strikes by communication workers and a nationwide stoppage by 90 000 oil workers in May (which had closed refineries and cut the fuel available for motoring and air lines). These had ended in concessions to the workers and gave encouragement for many similar confrontations of which that in the steel industry was merely the most prominent, carried out at the highest level and taken to law when the President attempted to take over the running of the steel mills—a manoeuvre which was rejected by the Supreme Court.

There was persistent comparison in the newspapers and over the radio of **price rises and wage increases**; in Britain the former failed to keep company with the latter. Since 1951 retail prices had gone up from an Index figure of 125 to 138 while the Index of Wages had risen from 119 to 129. Comparisons can be highly misleading and the following wages and prices are tentative. An agricultural worker was paid £5 13s (£5.65) for a 47 hour week—while a coal miner received £12 3s 9d (£12.17). **In the USA** a farm worker received about $5.40 per day and a miner $18.25.

Expenditure on food in rationed countries such as Britain was, of course, restricted. **A fairly typical weekly food bill** for a family of four in Britain might come to £3 or £4 per week; in the USA to $20. Expenditure on items other than food could vary considerably according to taste and habit. **Beer** cost about 1s 2d a pint (6p), in Britain where **rents** were, for the most part, curbed by the Rent Restriction Act of 1939. This system was open to abuse and often led to old houses falling into disrepair while new ones were in short supply. **Income Tax** at its maximum rate stood at 9s 6d (47p) in the £1, so that a married couple with two children might pay just over £111 per annum on an income of £1000.

Strikes caused inconvenience, and price rises and taxes were a daily source of vexation to millions of people, but probably took a lower place in their minds to the anxiety they felt for husbands, brothers and sons serving in the military forces, many of whom were engaged on active service. Not one of the major nations was without some sort of **compulsory National Service** seven years after the Second World War and, while the numerous theatres of

US police versus strikers

Casualties in Korea

war and trouble spots did not generate enormous casualty lists by the standards of 1939–45, there occurred the malignant dribble of deaths and injuries which, besides affecting individuals, crippled or pained the families of the afflicted. **For the USA,** heavily involved though it was on the United Nation's side in the **Korean War** (by 7 November they had suffered 127 000 casualties) there was no relief even though a new form of compulsory military service, intended in 1951 to replace the Selective Service Act (the Draft), and called the **Universal Military Service Act,** had been shelved by the House of Representatives on 4 March 1952 after it had been referred back to the Armed Services Committee. The original Act simply continued in force with the FBI in pursuit of about 5000 draft dodgers a year, the law sending some 600 to prison for two years while the rest were caught and inducted.

In Britain two years' military service was grudgingly accepted by the majority and positively enjoyed by the minority. Indeed, of the 872 000 in the three Services, 531 000 were regulars though many of these merely engaged in order to receive a much higher rate of pay. The Nation's volunteer spirit was far from dead and appeals to patriotism were by no means derided or rejected. Recruiting began on 28 April for the revived **Home Guard,** which had been disbanded at the end of the War. The target was 170 000 (later 91 000) each of whom was expected to carry out 60 hours training per annum. By the end of the year 25 000 had joined; the club spirit was strong even if the age level was a trifle high and equipment and uniforms in niggardly supply.

Dads' Army, second edition

Migration

Trends in the movements of populations continued to be on a large scale with far more wishing to shift their location from one country to another than the existing regulations permitted and future schemes seemed likely to encourage. Britain imposed few restrictions in those days so that many foreign workers, particularly of European origin, flowed in while a greatly increased number of about 200 000 left the country, nearly 18 000 of them to the USA. Movements within and out of Europe were extensive. The shift of population from East into West Germany increased to about 200 per day while, of the 202 000 Europeans who made up the 265 000 people permitted into the USA, 50 000 alone were Germans. Just over 2000 Jews per month were being attracted to Israel, though plans were initiated to admit them on a selective basis in order to consolidate the foundations of this new nation. Australia and New Zealand operated quota systems, with a preference for Britains over other Europeans, while South Africa witnessed as many people leaving as entering.

Transport, the choke which could impose unwanted restrictions on migration, presented few problems. Road and rail movement within the continents was simple except where strict frontier regulations imposed artificial barriers, particularly along the Iron Curtain in Europe (that was repeatedly brought to public attention by the news media and politicians) and the Bamboo Curtain 'erected' by China in the Far East. Passenger ships were in plentiful supply and the sale of passages was booming. Air transport, stimulated by bigger and faster airliners and cheaper fares, was beginning to play an important role.

Moreover, this far greater ease of travel was beginning to encourage a much larger number of people to take their holidays abroad, most of all among the Americans for whom the strength of the US Dollar on the International Money Markets was a boon.

Immigrants to the USA

Holidays

Holidays followed their traditional course, in so far as people went away or took time off when the weather was at its best, when the children were not at school or when national holidays were proclaimed. So July and August were the most popular months in the Northern Hemisphere. **The Americans poured into Europe** throughout most of the year and of the 350 000 who visited Europe,

170 000 came to Britain, of whom 42% travelled by air, encouraged by the new tourist fares with their 40–50% discount. They were not even put off by the undeniably inadequate and, in many places, scandalously poor hotel accommodation which suffered still from the aftermath of wartime restrictions, the annoyance of food rationing and a dire shortage of skilled staff. Income from tourism, nevertheless, was rated as Britain's best earner of foreign currency, some £110 million in all coming from 720 000 visitors, of which £41 million was in US dollars.

Tourists

For the Briton himself it had to be holidays at home of the pre-war pattern. **A foreign currency allowance** of only £25 per annum did not take him much further than Paris, and nothing like the extensive package tours of 25 years

The seaside holiday

later were in existence. Therefore, the advertisements in newspapers, magazines and guides were almost entirely for home resorts, the most adventurous coming from the Isle of Man which invited its patrons to 'Go Abroad this Year'. **Holiday Camps** were doing good business, their 'happy campers' seeming almost to relish the somewhat regimented routine to which they were made subject. At £5 per person per week with reductions for children it was quite a good package. Good value, too, seems to have been offered by the firm which advertised a 16 day cruising and coaching holiday in the Highlands of Scotland for £35; at least their customers would escape from the crowds. For the vast majority of holiday makers who wished to get away from home it was a case of packing their ration books, catching the bus or train to a seaside resort or, perhaps, one of the inland watering places like Harrogate ('Britain's Floral Resort', according to it's Information Bureau). They would stay in an hotel or boarding house and foray down to the beach each day and to the pub or to hear a band concert in the evening.

Homes

The homes the British occupied were in various states of repair, mostly mediocre, as the result of war-damage and inadequate materials. A new three bed-roomed house (about 1000 square ft floor space) might be purchased in some parts of the country for less than £2000, though a more general price was about £2500. Building Societies charged between $2\frac{1}{2}\%$ and $2\frac{3}{4}\%$. Unfortunately, less than 250 000 were being built every year (80% by local authorities) and the waiting list seemed as long as ever. Nevertheless, this construction effort by the British was a considerable achievement compared with **France**, for example, where only 45 000 new houses were built in 1951, or **Holland** where the annual figure was about 60 000. In the **USA**, on the other hand, there was no shortage for those who could afford to pay. Prices for houses over $15 000 were dropping and a mid-year estimate suggested that 25 000 of new houses, (20% of a year's total construction) remained unsold. So housing starts fell with the result that, in the autumn, federal controls on mortgages were removed and financing by the traditional sources was permitted again.

American suburbia

Furniture in Britain (as in most other countries) continued to copy traditional designs despite the publicity given to **avant-garde styles** which incorporated shiny metal, foam rubber and strange shapes. People mostly bought those pieces which looked functional and comfortable. They might pay £73 for a three-piece bedroom suite with another £10 for the double bed; or buy six Indian Tree pattern coffee cups and saucers for 16s 6d (83p); and a 10 ft 6 in × 9 ft Wilton carpet for £20.

Furniture in America

Food

Expenditure on food in Britain, as already mentioned, was somewhat curtailed by rationing, and food prices, of course, were officially controlled as well as distorted by subsidies. The cuts in subsidies announced in the Budget had the effect of adding $1\frac{1}{4}$d to a $1\frac{3}{4}$ lb loaf of bread, then costing 1s 3d (6p), and about 4d (2p) per lb on meat, raising the average cost of food per week per head of population by 1s 6d (7p). Typical of the approximate prices (and it is worth bearing in mind that, in the 25 years which have elapsed since 1952, there has been a four to five-fold multiplication of nearly all prices linked to the cost of living) being charged in the grocers shops were the following:

Butter	4s (20p) per lb rationed in July at 3oz per person per week
Milk	$6\frac{1}{2}$d (3p)
Meat	2s (10p) per lb rationed in July at 1s 9d (9p) per person per week
Bacon	4s (20p) per lb rationed in March at 5 oz per person per week
Pork Sausages	2s 6d (13p) per lb
Ground Rice	1s (5p) per lb
Tea	2s 6d (13p) rationed in July at $2\frac{1}{2}$ oz per person per week until 5 October when off ration
Cigarettes	1s $3\frac{1}{2}$d ($6\frac{1}{2}$p) for ten

As stated before, the weekly food bill for a family of four was about £3 10s (£3.50).

One year's meat ration for a family of four

Gardens

Most houses then being built were provided with gardens, and except in the most dense urban areas, they were, by the standards of 1977, lavish in size. Many people continued the wartime practice of growing food for themselves, and allotment gardens were also in high demand and well-cared for. Generally people spent quite a lot of time out-of-doors since television was, as yet, owned by relatively few people (for their preferences in entertainment see Section 4).

Health

Health standards were high in Britain, where the Health Service had been in full operation since 1948. Free medicine and treatment were beginning to pay a sound dividend as people became accustomed to visiting the doctor without the fear of crippling themselves financially. Indeed there were those who said the system was being abused by malingerers. Man's inborn interest in survival and medical science gave power to those who sought to spread its benefits. For example, the passing of the **Corneal Grafting Act** in June after a four year campaign by **B Rycroft**, enabled surgeons to remove eyes after death and restore the eyes of the living by a corneal graft without the fatally inhibiting need to indulge in prolonged legal wrangling. Since scars across the eyes accounted for $2\frac{1}{2}\%$ of blindness it meant that hundreds of people would benefit. On the other hand there was a lot of bickering over pay between those who ran the medical service and the doctors: this was resolved in April by an enquiry. The Conservative Government's proposal to **extend the charges for prescriptions** (at an annual saving of £2 million) gave deep offence to the Labour Party, which had sponsored the original Act. **Dental charges and hospital appliances** were to cost more, as well, although dental examinations would remain free.

Cancer which caused an increasing number of deaths and which, by comparison with successful preventitive measures against other diseases, seemed all the more alarming, came in for a high degree of publicity in 1952. The publication by the World Health Organisation of a statistical study of the disease showed not only that the incidence of death had risen in 50 years from about 5% to 11%, in some countries, it also focused ones attention on indications that **smoking might be an important cause of lung cancer,** which had shown a spectacular increase. **It is from this moment that the campaign against smoking began.** In the USA, where Government assistance in the medical field was not so comprehensive as in Britain and the more Socialist states, over $16 million was subscribed to the **American Cancer Society**, of which $4 million was committed to research.

To the forefront in public anxiety about health was the control of **poliomyelitis** (infantile paralysis) some forms of which had crippling effects on children. In Britain there were only about 5000 cases in 1952 compared with nearly 8000 in 1950, which was the worst year on record so far. In Europe, however, there was a severe outbreak, the worst epidemic being centred on **Copenhagen** with 3000 cases in a four month period, of which one in eight was seriously paralysed. **In the USA** there was more than a doubling of cases from the 25 500 of 1951 to over 52 000, with more than 4000 in a single week at one time. Experimental inoculations with **gamma globulin** and **gelatin** in the USA were as yet inconclusive, such hopes as they raised seeming merely to produce a modification of its effect's severity.

Accidents occurred with their normal incidence throughout the year with the exception of those associated with road traffic. As the number of road vehicles and their speeds increased the death and injury bill went up in proportion. **In the USA the number of road deaths** was up 3% on the 23 770 of 1951. Driving while under the influence of drink was a known cause of many accidents and a device (called an **intoximeter** in 1941) was patented in 1952 by **Glenn Forrester** (USA). Additionally there was a **drunkometer** devised by **R Harger** and an **alcoholmeter** by **Professors Greenberg** and **Keator** of Yale University.

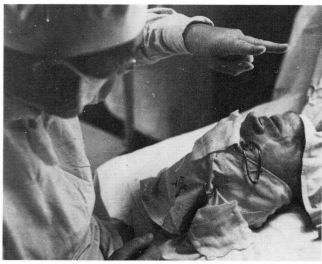

Cornea grafting

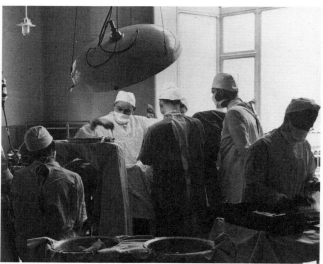

The operating theatre

It was the drunkometer which, in 1952, brought about the first conviction, in Chicago, by this method.

Animal health could at times have a very close and direct effect upon individuals. In many parts of the world, for example, rabies could easily be contracted from domestic animals let alone the wild kind. Less direct in

Treating a ewe for maggot-fly

their immediate effects, though widespread in their impact on food supply, were the diseases that struck farm animals. **Foot and mouth disease** was the one most noticeable in the USA and Canada, but particularly in Britain where outbreaks were controlled by the isolation and slaughter of the entire infected herds. In this respect 1952 was a bad year for Britain as the outbreak, which had begun in Eastern Europe in 1951, was spreading steadily westwards to become the worst for ten years. No less than £1.5 million worth of livestock was slaughtered in Great Britain in the first six months of the year as the result of 430 incidents, but by the middle of August the worst was over. Thereupon **fowl pest** began to take its toll in October and continued with widespread outbreaks for the rest of the year. **Denmark**, however, achieved a truly remarkable feat in 1952 by **completing the total elimination of tuberculosis in her cattle**, an event which was at once apparent in the reduction of tuberculosis in Danish children, with such a decline in demand on her sanatoriums that room could be found to treat foreigners.

The harvest in Britain was above the average for most crops, the cattle population fell a little and the number of men working the land dropped by 4%—a characteristic wastage as more machines took over. In Europe and the USA, too, agricultural products reached high levels. In the USA 27.5 million head of cattle and 85 million head of pigs were slaughtered of which no less than 94% went to feed indigenous people, making the USA among the greatest meat eating nations in the world with consumption at 177 lb per person per annum. Prices remained steady for the farmer, though his net return was down on previous years in the USA. Prices of land per acre in Britain stood between £50 and £100 in the rural areas.

In India, however, where the population increased by nearly 2%, the production of cereal crops fell even though the harvest was good, the reason being a decline in the acreage under use. So this vast nation which was not self-

A good harvest

supporting and also short of foreign currency, lived perenially close to famine and depended on big injections of foreign aid, mainly from the USA, the Colombo Plan and the International Bank.

Education

For the Education Services of the world this was a year of crisis at a time of approval for vast plans of expansion when resources and prejudices tended to hold them back while the number of students increased. **In Britain and most other countries** the schools were held back by the shortage of resources in money, suitable premises and trained teachers. At a time of financial crisis in Britain a three month freeze on new construction had been applied in December 1951 and this affected every activity, including teacher training which went on in almost any sort of accommodation from old stately homes and institutions to hutments. There was a dire shortage of woman teachers. **Even in the wealthy USA** there was relatively financial stringency, though here politics and racial problems were the main cause. Though President Truman had asked for federal aid to meet 'the crisis in the schools', as he called it, a Congress hostile to him virtually vetoed his efforts, although in March it did pump additional funds into building. It was estimated that one in eight persons receiving public education suffered from inadequate facilities. **Those who suffered most were the negroes** whose case for desegregation was due to be heard by the Supreme Court early in 1952, only to be deferred until December. Nevertheless, national conscience and propaganda was already creating an improvement for the negroes. The Supreme Court ruling in the crucial case of

Brown v Plessey was not finally delivered until 1954, a turning point on the question of Educational discrimination in the USA.

Homework in Harlem

The availability and cost of books, be they for education or relaxation, was, from the commercial point of view, good. Both in the USA and Britain the number of new editions and turnover was up while prices had levelled off at an average of 13s 8d (68p) per copy. (As to the quality of their contents, see Section 4). There was every hope that the writers themselves would benefit from the **UNESCO Universal Copyright Convention**, signed by 43 countries at Geneva on 6 September, to which the USA adhered in 1954 and Britain in 1957, and to which Russia and China, among others, were not signatories at that time. Educational books figured high in the list of bestsellers, though never publicised as such, and accounted for a very large slice of the considerable British export trade in books (Turnover of all British books was over £42 million of which exports were £14 million).

Religion

The religious movements continued their stately course with the **Church of England** seeming to be as much concerned about death watch beetle in the ancient timbers of its cathedrals as about its declining congregations. For this was a year which produced many appeals but hardly any great reformative initiatives. Indeed, the Church of England was on the defensive when the Archbishop of Canterbury was compelled to explain the activities of his Dean, **Dr Hewlett Johnson—'The Red Dean'**—for upholding Chinese claims that the United Nations had used bacteriological warfare in Korea. **In China** the Western religious missions were being steadily extinguished by the Communist regime and the **Communist electoral successes in Kerala**, southern India, were credited to the enormous quantities of Communist literature which had swamped Christian propaganda. To combat Communism the religious organisations stepped up their production of literature and its distribution to the places where literacy was being extended and education was booming.

The Red Dean

The Law

Linked to publishing, in Britain there was enacted a new **Defamation Act** (introduced by **Harold Lever**) which gave improved protection to authors in cases of accidental defamation and clearer definition to a vexed subject. It also laid down that defamation during a radio broadcast was always libel, not slander (although spoken). Quite the most interesting court cases were those involving **Apartheid** in South Africa and **Iran's oil** (See Section 1), but otherwise 1952 was not a year of major amendment to the principles of law or its implementation. The British Army came more closely into line, however, when the **Court Martial Appeal Act** of 1951 was brought into effect. An early case demonstrated, what had long been apparent in military circles, that evidence did not always justify the verdict and that the previous Review Procedure had been inadequate. **It was in the USA where the highest administration of law was in serious difficulty**. In the

Supreme Court, where a majority vote was needed, disagreements led to an extensive diversity of opinion (no less than six times on the issue of the steel industry seizure case). Much time was spent in consideration of Immigration (referred to above). In one instance it authorised deportation, under the anti-Communist provisions of the Alien Registration Act of 1940, of three people who had entered the country 30 years previously and had not applied for naturalisation. In this instance, as in others, the Supreme Court may have demonstrated its sensitivity to public opinion, for at this moment justice in the USA was being perverted by a witch hunt led by **Senator Joseph McCarthy**. Since 1950, McCarthy,

Joseph McCarthy

a colourful individual who has been described as the most effective demagogue in American history, had acquired a terrifying reputation on congressional committees for harrying communists—be they real or imagined. With a large national following baying at his heels, he was difficult to combat, though **Senator William Benton** was fearless in his opposition and withstood a $2 million action for libel, slander and conspiracy filed by McCarthy. Even **Dwight Eisenhower**, as he stood for President, felt the need for caution in commenting on the Senator from Wisconsin, in case his own prospects were damaged. **Senator John Kennedy**, during his successful attempt to defeat **Representative Cabot Lodge** in the November elections, was distinctly equivocal on the subject. In the meantime the careers of many leading people from all walks of life were thrown into jeopardy by a technique of vituperative and unproven accusations that were the antithesis of natural justice.

Money

The pronounced addiction of people to gamble rather than take calculated risks is never more clearly indicated than by the annual publication of the statistics of betting. In the USA there was a 19% increase over 1951 on **horse race betting** through pari-mutuel devices (the 'tote', in which $1939 million was invested). Bookmakers were unusually cautious over the odds on Dwight Eisenhower winning the Presidential election (having burnt their fingers over **Thomas Dewey's** failure, against the odds, to win in 1948) and discouraged by a Federal Law from 1951 which compelled them to buy a $50 tax stamp. In Philadelphia the US District Court ruled against that law, objecting to it as a police measure enacted under the guise of a tax bill and an intrusion on state rights. For the most part the law was accepted. The immense gambling empire at **Las Vegas, Nevada,** which had been made possible when gambling previously was legalised, increased in size and scope.

Perhaps the greatest increase of gambling in any country was recorded by France where it was up 29% over 1951. The general trend in most advanced countries was upward, a trend which became more pronounced as the financial climate improved towards the end of the year.

In Britain the largest total of money was invested in **Football Pools** (about 4s (20p) per person taking part) and 30% was extracted by the Treasury by way of tax. Even so Shermans claimed the **world's largest Seven Match Treble Chance** pool with a dividend of £45 286 to 1s (5p) and Littlewoods and Vernons topped that with a few £75 000 payouts. The Treasury reaped the benefit of £28 million in betting taxation against the estimated £540 million invested, which itself was a little under 1% of average national personal expenditure.

Stockbrokers

On the world's two dominant Stock Markets, those of the USA and Britain, the price trend was marginally upwards despite, in the USA, severe industrial unrest and, in Britain, the underlying dollar crisis and recession. In the USA the **Standard and Poor Index** rose by about ten points on the year with dividend yields in the region of 5.8% on Ordinary stocks. In Britain Ordinary shares, which fell sharply from 121 in January to 110 in February, had come back to 117 by December with dividends yields steady at 5.8%. In effect, this was not a very dramatic year for the amateur punter in shares: with the markets so relatively lifeless even the professionals were hard put to make fortunes.

Poolwinners (£75 000 each) with Maurice Chevalier

People in Britain had **the urge to save** deeply impressed upon them. The Savings Campaigns, which had been so prominent during the war, continued with little slackening. Local papers printed league tables showing which communities had reached their savings targets. Nevertheless, National Savings fell throughout the year, withdrawals exceeding deposits by £81 million even though the maximum amount that might be invested in the Post Office Savings Bank was raised from £2000 to £3000 per person and the permissable number of Saving Certificates put up from 500 to 700. People were feeling the financial pinch and an interest rate of between $2\frac{1}{2}\%$ to 4% on Government Bonds, whose capital value was falling in value with inflation, no longer attracted them as once was the case. The incentive of patriotism, though called upon, failed to have quite the same force in this respect.

Industrial man

SECTION 3

THE WORLD OF MACHINES

Ships

The most exciting ship to enter service in 1952 was, beyond doubt, the United States Lines liner, *United States*. Built for the North Atlantic passenger trade in competition with those other great ships already operating to full capacity on that route, she was the fastest liner in the world though, at 53 300 tons, not the biggest. That distinction still belonged to the 83 673 ton *Queen Elizabeth*. The general expectation that she would capture the Blue Ribbon Trophy for the Atlantic crossing was duly satisfied on her maiden voyage: from New York to Europe she averaged 35.59 knots to complete the outward voyage in 3 days 10 hours 40 minutes and averaged 34.51 knots on the return voyage which took 3 days 12 hours 12 minutes to beat the previous records which had been held by the *Queen Mary* since 1938. Those records stand to this day and mark the zenith of the era of passenger liners prior to their decline under mounting competition from air transport. The significant marine innovation of the year came with the announcement of positive plans to build **nuclear powered warships** (see Section 1) with the promise also (largely unfulfilled as it happens) of a revolution in sea transport practice.

The first car (a Daimler) leaves the Lord Warden

Shipbuilding, world wide, continued at a high level throughout the year as the inroads caused by war time losses were largely made good. On 30 September, for example, British shipbuilders had 7 million tons on their order books, even though new orders were less than they had been the year before. Although there was concern that sufficient steel would not be made available to meet

SS United States *arrives in Southampton for the first time*

demand, these were heydays for the British industry which far out-built all foreign competitors. In Scotland, on 22 January, the four diesel engined 12 500 ton tanker *Auris* made its first voyage fitted with **the world's first merchant ship's gas turbine engine** in lieu of one of the diesels—a 1200 hp unit which, without assistance, could propel the ship at 7 knots. There were not many other innovations in that year as far more attention was being concentrated by ship-owners on efforts to rationalise their fleets into economic units composed mostly of new oil burners. **Freight rates** were, overall, lower and more shipping was laid up. An under-current of disputes in numerous ports added to costs. **Dock labour forces** tended to grow less, a trend that was given further impetus when Britain's first roll-on—roll-off ferry, *The Lord Warden*, came into cross Channel service for 120 cars on 5 May.

Mishaps at sea are mentioned in Section 8 while the saga of the *Flying Enterprise* in January is recorded in Section 1. Inevitably there were technical troubles, though only with the more prestigious ships did they come to public notice—as with the new 20 300 ton French liner *Flandre* which made her maiden Atlantic voyage in mid-July and then had to be taken out of service until the following year because of serious mechanical trouble.

Crusader *at speed*

Boats

The most sensational boating incident of the year centred upon attempts to exceed 200 mph. In July **Stanley Sayres** of the USA had established the record at 178.49 mph in the hydroplane *Slo-Mo-Shun IV*, but he was challenged in September by Britain's **John Cobb** in **the first jet-propelled contender for the record**, *Crusader*, which was driven by a 5000 lb thrust engine. Having failed to beat Sayres in mid-month, Cobb, whose fame was founded on land speed records and who was the holder of the world land speed record, set out on 29 January on Loch Ness. On the first run he clocked 206.89 mph but, while travelling at about 240 mph on the reciprocal leg of the measured mile, the boat hit some ripples crossing her course and she began to pitch. Then, as she slowed, the bows plunged under, the boat disintegrated and Cobb was killed.

John Cobb

Aircraft and Rockets

Apart from the main aeronautical feats related in Section 1 there were several events, detached from conventional record breaking, that gave insight into the future. On 20 November **Captain J Slade Nash**, of the US Air Force, pushed up the speed record to 698.50 mph flying in a North American F 86D Sabre fighter. At the negative end of the power scale, **Philip Wills** of Britain won the world gliding championships at Madrid out of a field of 56 competitors from 18 countries, setting up in the process a new British altitude record for 22 430 ft. In the USA a world speed record for gliding was set by **Richard Johnson** at 53.8 mph. Gliding now began to invade the frontiers of discovery, for 1952 was the year of intrigued, initial public discussion of **'jet streams'**—air currents of 300 mph that blew in altitudes (between 25 and 40 000 ft) which could influence high flying aircraft and, perhaps, lift gliders to undreamt of altitudes.

The use of rockets in the upper atmosphere also began to attract far greater attention after the few years lull which had followed their advent as military weapons in German hands. Mr **Duncan Sandys** announced in July that guided anti-aircraft rockets—'these fantastic weapons'—were now an assured reality, while contemporary commentaries began to admit that the **space age**—this 'half serious project'—was closer than some thought possible. The second International Congress of Astronautics described as 'most feasible' the idea of **orbitting stations** with ion rockets plying between them. Nearer to immediate reality came news of a highly sophisticated twin jet aircraft, the USA's *XA-25*, with a rumoured capability of climbing to 200 000 ft, and reaching speeds approaching 2000 mph—a target which was later achieved with something to spare but which, at the time, seemed to border on the incredible.

Closer to earth, the very apparent success of **helicopters** in Malaya and, in supporting land forces at war, most of all, Korea, gave stimulating impetus to this type of machine. As a means of evacuating casualties from the battlefield they assumed a sort of 'angel of mercy' image, but their equally important characteristics as commercial vehicles also drew attention. **The first cross Atlantic flight by this sort of machine** was completed in five 'legs'

The F 86D Sabre fighter

A US rocket experiment firing monkeys and mice into space from New Mexico

First helicopters across the Atlantic

on 31 July, when two US *Sikorsky S-55s* arrived at Prestwick in Scotland, having covered the 3410 miles from the USA in 42½ hours' flying time at an average

speed of 80 mph. In Britain the Fairey Company said that it was going ahead with a jet powered, 40-seater helicopter with a speed of 200 mph—*the Rotodyne*.

The year 1952 was rich in the appearance or projection of aircraft which were to become famous because of the extremes of their technical achievements, or as trail blazers in the search for reliable and safe commercial aircraft. The following list provides names that, 25 years later, have become household names or which have long since passed into oblivion:

BRITAIN

The *Comet* **four-jet airliner** which launched **the world's first jet liner service**. The *Avro 698* (*Vulcan*) four jet bomber—the first Delta winged bomber which is still in RAF service, though a trifle obsolescent. *The Handley-Page HP 80* (*Victor*) four jet bomber with its crescent wing, of which some still do useful service as tanker aircraft for flight refuelling. The *Bristol Britannia* four turbo-propeller airliner.

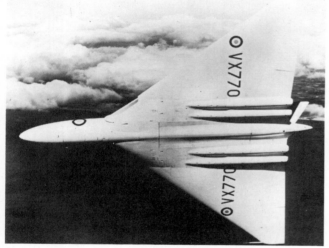

The Avro Vulcan

FRANCE

The night-fighter version of the *Dassault Mystère*

HOLLAND

The *Fokker F-27* (*Friendship*) twin turbo-propellor airliner (in mock-up).

USSR

Information at this time was very sparse, but first sightings took place of a new jet fighter, the *Mig-19*, as successor to the *Mig-15* that was so active over the Korean war fronts.

USA

The *Boeing YB 52* (*Strato-fortress*) an eight-engined jet bomber with the heaviest bomb-load operational bomber of all times (75 000 lb).

The *Douglas XA 3D-1* (*Skywarrior*) twin-jet naval attack aircraft.

With aircrafts' ranges of operation known to be increasing, wide publicity was also given to the practice of flight-refuelling and notably some long distance flights by RAF *Canberra* twin-jet bombers. While these ventures were mainly military in their application, something far

more important from the commercial angle took place on 19/20 November when a *Douglas DC 6* of Scandinavian Air System **pioneered the air route across the North Pole**, from Los Angeles to Copenhagen, carrying a crew of thirteen, 500 lb of mail and, as a safety measure, Arctic survival equipment. The journey was in three stages with refuelling stops at Edmonton and the recently opened US air base of Thule in Greenland. It covered 5853 miles (1000 miles shorter than the normal route via New York) and took 28 hours 7 minutes, including more than 4 hours on the ground. On 1 May **the first trans-Atlantic tourist fares came into operation costing 30% less than 1st class fares**.

First airliner over the North Pole

Rail and Tramways

So far as most railways were concerned, the early 1950s appeared very similar to previous decades since, although electric and oil-fired locomotives were to be found in many parts of the world, many were still fuelled by coal which, particularly in Britain, was much cheaper than oil. Nevertheless, even in Britain a positive movement towards liquid-fuelled locomotives was made manifest by the appearance of the **first British-built gas-turbine locomotive**, the 3000 hp 130 ton Metro-Vic. (A Swiss-built type had been running in Britain throughout 1951). Claimed as the most powerful locomotive on British rail, it was capable of drawing a 650 ton train at speeds up to 90 mph and was much simpler to operate and maintain than its traditional steam competitors. At the same time orders for diesel-engines to replace obsolete steam locomotives was announced. Weight-saving also became a more conscious preoccupation among designers at this time. The subject was illuminated when London Transport brought 90 aluminium coaches into service, a

The Metro-Vic gas-turbine locomotive

departure from the steel type and the target for a certain amount of criticism related to safety in the event of a crash. For 1952 also brought England's worst ever rail accident, when a double collision involved three trains at Harrow and Wealdstone station (see Section 8) killing 112 people.

The implementation of safety had been paramount in railway operation since their inception and the first ever fatal crash in 1830. Numerous improvements to signalling systems had been introduced over the years with a gradual movement towards automation and the elimination of human error such as had caused the Harrow crash. **The first push-button route-selecting signalling control system in Britain** was brought into service by London Transport in November, while in October trials had begun of an experimental automatic system, whereby a bell was rung in the driver's cab if a signal was clear, a hooter sounded if at caution when simultaneously a partial application of the brakes was made.

While new systems were still under development, the actual track mileage of the world's largest system continued its steady decline: in the USA it was decreasing by about 1000 miles per annum at an accelerating rate. This was only marginally the case in Britain, though the railways' cousin, street tramways, were fast disappearing. On 5 July **the last London tram made its final journey** and buses took over. On the other hand, the seaside town of Blackpool put a brand new fleet of trams into service, which still runs 25 years later.

Most interesting of rail experiments was a new variation of the single rail system, a train running on a **mono-rail** centred in a raised concrete track. Tried in Germany and called the *Alwegbahn*, it was of Swedish design with a claimed potential maximum speed of 200 mph, but like so many mono-rail systems it made little headway.

Road Transport

Just as sea transport was beginning in 1952 to feel the first pinch of competition from air transport, so were the railways becoming increasingly aware of the threat from lorries and cars which had been partially arrested due to the war. The ending of petrol rationing in Britain in 1950 had strongly stimulated automobile growth, and a rise of 7½d (3p) per gallon in the Budget merely took petrol to 4s 3d (21p) per gallon, a price that was not in the least penal. At the same time the tax rating on horse-power for cars was changed to a flat rate of £12 10s (£12.50) per annum to the encouragement of those who hoped to own more powerful cars. Though, world wide, the rate of increase for road transport was rapid, it's growth rate had slowed in the USA from 6% in 1951 to 3% due to shortage of materials, slacker demand and higher prices. In France, Italy and Germany it increased but in Britain production fell because of a quota system geared to the materials available and, particularly, shortages in steel: 432 000 cars (between 60 and 70% of capacity) were produced in 1952, compared with 476 000 in 1951, and only 312 000 were exported compared with 369 000 the year before. Attacking interferance from officialdom, **Mr Lord**, deputy chairman of the **British Motor Corporation**, warned that, if certain controls were not removed, the spectre of unemployment might stalk the country. But at the same time many doubts were being expressed about the efficiency of management in the industry.

There were few innovations of vital importance from the technical point of view, although **the first attempt at commercial production of a fibre glass body** was a landmark after years of experiment.

In European motor racing the field was dominated by the Italian firm of **Ferrari** which was practically unchallenged. The feeble display of the first British **BRM,**

The Ferrari's top driver, A Ascari

Below: *Fibre-glass bodies for sports cars*

which failed at every outing, was compensated by the achievement of British sports cars. An **Allard** won the Monte Carlo Rally; **Jowetts** took the 1500 cc class at Le Mans; **Sunbeam-Talbots** dominated the Alpine Rally (one of their drivers being **Stirling Moss**) and a **Jaguar XK 120,** driven by a team of four drivers headed by Moss, averaged more than 100 mph for 17 days and nights, covering 16 851 miles at Montlhéry, with Moss taking the fastest circuit at 121.28 mph. In America **the Indianapolis 500 mile** event was won in a **Agajaman Special** driven by **Troy Ruttman** at a record average speed of 128.92 mph.

In Motor Cycle racing the honours were mostly shared, fairly evenly, between the British and Italians, with **Geoffrey Duke** riding **Nortons** as the outstanding British rider. A Norton also won the US championship at Daytona beach. In the world Markets British machines were in the vast majority, earning about £45 million in export orders and sweeping aside all competition. However, that year a new threat began to appear from Japan, where machines were being marketed, in some cases, with badges that looked remarkably like those of their British competitors.

Reg Armstrong winning the Senior TT at the Isle of Man on a Norton

Nor was there much in the way of innovation in manifestations of **commercial transport** which continued to expand as roads were improved and more lorries became available. Almost everywhere, except in Britain, roads were built or improved while ambitious plans were laid for the future. The Western European nations agreed on a system of trans-European highways; a motorway to Brussels was going ahead; great schemes were being hatched in Japan; while in the USA, where two in every three families had a car, the greatest number of projects of all proceeded with an annual expenditure of about $4500 million for new construction and maintenance. In Britain everybody complained about road safety and the threat of traffic jams, but the central

debate revolved around **denationalisation of road transport**, a Bill to this effect being introduced in July. Public opinion was in favour of the measure in the proportion of about 48–39% and at the end of the year, although legislation was not yet complete, it was fairly certain that the Government's proposals would be carried.

Electronics, Mechanisation and Machine Tools

While the industrialised world was engaged in an intensive search for **new ways of implementing automation** with a view to cost-cutting and labour-saving (among, other motives) there existed at least one opinion that the economic life of Britain was 'seriously affected by malaise periodically sharpened by crises', a view which was fitfully shared by a majority. In British coalmines, where about 75% of cutting was done by machines, some 97% of coal was still loaded by hand. However, the farms of Britain with one tractor per 23 hectares of arable land, were the most highly mechanised in the world, those of the USA coming second at 48. In fact British scientists and researchers, along with those from other countries, were playing a prominent role in the search for new ideas. Progress was being made with the development of the **revolutionary transistors** (invented in 1947) that would eventually largely supercede thermionic valves. The earliest computers were being sophisticated and put to new imaginative purposes. For example, transistors were adapted to work at high frequencies and the **ENIAC computer** in the USA was programmed for

The ENIAC computer

the first time by semi-permanent wiring and a card-reader employed. A computer called **RAYDA** was used to analyse the behaviour of rockets in flight, while another was being developed by American Airlines to handle the booking of tickets. Meanwhile in Britain a report was made about the results obtained from experiments with all-electronic telephone exchanges, using thermionic valves, and in the USA it was revealed that an airborne electronic device was being employed to detect radiations from atomic explosions. There was discussion, too, of using computers to analyse information that would assist **in long range weather forecasting.**

Automation, first called by that name in 1936, invaded an increasing number of activities, and exhibitions of the latest machine-tools held in London and in Hanover demonstrated their possibilities for copying processes. The problem of cutting such tough substances as tungsten carbide, diamonds and glass was tackled by a new ultrasonic process by vibrating a soft tool at high frequency and low amplitude against the material while a mixture of water and abrasive material was passed round and under the tool.

Heavy Engineering and Power Supply

Apart from shipbuilding and road making, the largest engineering projects, which repeatedly stimulated public imagination, were those connected with the electricity supply industry. The vast outlay and mechanical activity associated with acquiring raw materials, iron-ore, coal, oil and the like, which were part of an ancient process, slipped into obscurity in comparison with **great hydro-electric schemes** and the construction of the **latest power stations.** The demand for electric power in Britain (rising at about 8% per annum) was linked to the public debate connected with full utilisation of coal which, even at £5 13s (£5.65) per ton for house coal, was considered by harassed (and rationed) householders expensive. Demand for electric fires was suppressed, however, by a Purchase Tax of 100% levied upon them. Nevertheless 1952 was the year when the **first thermal storage heaters** using off-peak electricity were introduced. By way of experiment the **first British Metro-Vick gas-turbine generator**, giving 15 000 kw, was started at Trafford, small wind generators were erected in Scotland and, most important of all, the Atomic Energy Research Establishment began serious work on a project which, in 1956 at Calder Hall (and practically on schedule as planned in 1952) became the **world's first large-scale operational reactor power plant.**

Development chiefly concentrated upon familiar and well-proven methods using familiar fuels. In Britain it was decided to build power stations on coalfields to use coal that might otherwise be unsaleable. In Canada, linked to the projected **St Lawrence Seaway** (a joint scheme with the USA), tenders were invited for the construction of a hydro-plant that would eventually generate 2.2 million hp. **The most ambitious hydro-plant in Europe took a step forward when the Donzère-Mondragon power station**, that was part of the enormous development scheme down the Rhône Valley, was opened by the President of France on 25 October. Linked to a system of navigational canals and locks which actually diverted the original course of the river and significantly added to its commercial use, the power station would eventually create about 420 000 hp and generate 300 Mw. In Scotland extensive tunnelling was in progress for the hydro-electric schemes at **Loch Quoich, the River Conon and Glen Moriston**. In the USA work was completed on the 5 mile long tunnel for a new hydro-electric station at **Niagara Falls**. In Australia the initial tunnelling began for the highly ambitious **Snowy Mountain scheme**. But the biggest hydro-electric plant

Hydro-electric plant in Scotland

in the world came into full production in March at **Harsprånget** in Sweden, a 350 Mw project installed in a cavern excavated from solid rock. The entire complex was one of advanced innovation—from the excavations to the electric control devices used and the successful employment of an ultra-high tension transmission system which many experts had feared might fail.

In complete contrast, an **electric wrist watch** was shown at Chicago, by the Elgin National Watch Company, powered by a $\frac{1}{2}$ in long, pencil slim battery, and claimed as capable of keeping perfect time while running for a year.

Work on the Donzère-Mondragon project

The 280 mm cannon

Weapons

In a world committed to extensive rearmament, it was inevitable that many new machines were designed to be used exclusively as, or in association with, weapons of war; certain types of aeroplane and warship have been mentioned already. Probably the most sinister, as well as among the largest of land warfare machines, was the **280 mm cannon** unveiled to the public in September by the US Army. This enormous piece, which weighed 85 tons, was carried from one place to another at speeds up to 35 mph, suspended between two 500 hp prime-movers and could be brought into action within only a few minutes. It could fire a conventional shell weighing 750 lb to a range of about 20 miles, but it was mainly required as an **atomic cannon** though, as yet, it had still to fire that kind of projectile.

The debate over future atomic warfare overlay almost everything in military discussion, and therefore the series of tests, that took place in the Nevada Desert USA throughout the year, aroused enormous public interest, particularly when they were seen on television from coast to coast, as they were for the first time on 22 April. Six cameras carried the pictures to a vast audience. Further tests went on throughout the spring and summer, in some of which troops on the ground were placed in fairly close proximity to ground zero.

Apart from atomics, few new weapons of great significance were announced even though extensive work was proceeding to develop the latest range of vehicles, ships, aircraft and armaments initiated since the war. For example, security was so tight that it was only on 31 March that the Royal Navy unveiled the **Squid anti-submarine weapon**, which they had possessed and used in the latter stages of the Second World War. This was an electronically controlled triple-barrelled mortar, capable of firing 500 lb finned depth charges ahead of the parent ship or far to the beam in response to information received from the latest sonar detection device. While the Soviet Russian orientated nations used relatively few makes of weapon (because they were largely standardised on Russian designs) the NATO allies had developed a proliferation of different national types which made initial co-operation very difficult. Many proposals were made in public debate—besides behind closed doors—to achieve standardisation by calibre sizes and vehicles if in nothing else. However, nothing concrete appeared in 1952 or for many years to come, though in the British Army, at least, the year was to see the virtual completion of its programme to equip with the **Centurion tank**, which had proven itself so well in Korea as the best tank then in service in any army.

Agriculture

Though to the casual observer the most noticeable aspect of farm mechanisation appeared in the shape of tractors, combines and machinery in the fields, there was one important new device introduced which gave hope that **mechanised milking** might soon be extended to every farm. In Britain it was the cows of the large herds that were milked mechanically. A machine costing about £100 and providing the 'Cow to Churn' system, offered the possibility of economic mechanical milking for the many smaller herds.

SECTION 4
THE ENTERTAINMENT BUSINESS

Theatre

As a generalised reflection upon a year of political and economic uncertainty, it is reasonable to say that 1952 was denied the sight of anything startlingly original in the way of play, playwrite, actor or actress while the one **play which was to have the longest single run of any other in history** merely received a routine mention. Theatres in the USA were bedevilled by a vicious rise in costs and in Britain by the paucity of audiences. Indeed, in Europe it was Germany alone which benefited by a genuine theatrical boom.

Two American dramatists, **Jeanette Dowling** and **Francis Letton**, caught the popular imagination (fortuitously associated with a new Queen in Britain) with their *The Young Elizabeth*, in which the talented **Mary Morris** suddenly emerged from years of personal disappointment to join the ranks of the celebrities. Another American actress to make a hit on the London Stage was film star **Katherine Hepburn** in Shaw's *The Millionairess*. In the USA **John van Druten**'s *I am a Camera* (built upon some short stories by **Christopher Isherwood**) won the author and **Julie Harris** (who played Sally Bowles) the New York Drama Critics Prize. Musical comedy in the USA, for the most part, depended upon old favourites such as *South Pacific* and *Guys and Dolls*, while *Call me Madam* received a rapturous reception in London with **Billie Worth** and **Anton Walbrook** in the title roles, the

Mary Morris as the young Elizabeth

Billie Worth and Anton Walbrook in 'Call me Madam'

latter giving a remarkable performance of toneless singing.

There was the usual batch of revivals with **Rodgers and Hart**'s *Pal Joey* taking pride of place in the USA and **Alan Badel, Claire Bloom** and **Athene Seyler** dominating the Shakespeare season in Britain by their outstanding performances in *Romeo and Juliet* at the Old Vic. There were plays, too, from nearly all the best established writers—**J B Priestley**'s experimental venture, *The Dragon's Mouth*; **Noel Coward**'s *Quadrille*; **Terence Rattigan**'s *The Deep Blue Sea*; **Charles Morgan**'s *The River Line*; **Bertolt Brecht**'s *Der gute Mensch von Sezuam*; and **Anita Loos**'s adaptation of **Simone Colette**'s *Gigi* among the successes.

Both in London and New York pride of place for a first class murder mystery went to **Frederick Knott**'s *Dial M for Murder*, a play which often bears repetition 25 years later. But opening at the 453 seater Ambassador's Theatre on 25 November was a play by **Agatha Christie**, produced by **Peter Cotes** with **Richard Attenborough** and **Sheila Sim** in the star roles, which runs to this day. It was called *The Mousetrap* and was summed up by one critic as ... 'having prospects of success', while the *Times* wrote that, 'The piece admirably fulfills the special requirements of the theatre' and mentioned ... 'the alarming silences which are perhaps the true test of such a piece on the stage.'

Sheila Sim and Richard Attenborough

Cinema

The competition generated from the vastly increased number of television sets in people's homes was having a significant effect upon the cinema industry. TV's impact (see below) was most noticeable in the USA where the number of sets had risen from 1.5 million in 1949 to 18 million in 1952, and the number of feature films produced had fallen from 363 to 278 in those years respectively. The riposte, led by Hollywood, took the form of a considerable increase in expenditure in presentation and technology with emphasis on the gigantic rather than on improved quality of story and acting. Supreme examples of this policy were the first public showing of the much publicised wide screen, devised by three projectors with synchronised sound and called **This is Cinerama** (which had been invented as long ago as 1937) and the introduction of Eastman Color material with its improved colour

A model of the Cinerama theatre

Danny Kaye and Hans Christian Anderson

reproduction that encouraged many more film makers to adopt colour instead of black and white, and in years to come led to the virtual elimination of the black and white picture. As for extravagance, the record for the year was held by Metro-Goldwyn-Mayer with its $4 million production *Hans Christian Anderson* in Technicolor starring **Danny Kaye**, a film which broke a 16 year record for first week box office takings in New York and helped justify those who believed that the star system and vast outlay were the proper way to compete with television. Yet the relatively cheap *High Noon*, written by **Carl Foreman**, produced by **Stanley Kramer** and starring **Gary Cooper**, was to become a classic Western, which to this day remains memorably fresh for its quality and was to win Academy Awards besides showing a handsome profit. Likewise, **Charles Chaplin**'s *Limelight*, starring himself and **Claire Bloom**, achieved success on artistic merit besides nostalgia and star appeal. Academy Awards undeniably produced results that did not necessarily reflect full satisfaction at the box office. The 1952

awards for films made in 1951 seemed to place emphasis on *A Street Car Named Desire* in which **Marlon Brando** made his name (without winning an award): in all this film collected four awards (including Best Actress for **Vivien Leigh**), but it was well down the list of attractions for those cinema goers who preferred films such as *The African Queen* with **Humphrey Bogart** (Academy Best Actor) and **Katherine Hepburn**; and musicals such as *An American in Paris* with **Gene Kelly** which also won four awards in connection with art, presentation and music.

European films and the stars they introduced were in a strict minority, though far from ignored by Hollywood. For the British film industry, 1952 was a singularly poor year, with *Mandy* outstanding among a poor lot, but in France **René Clair** produced *Les Belles du Nuit* and, in so doing, firmly imprinted the image of the beautiful **Gina Lollobrigida** in the eyes and minds of film audiences as she set out on the international phase of her career.

Chaplin and Bloom in 'Limelight'

Gary Cooper in 'High Noon'

Humphrey Bogart on the 'African Queen' set

Lollobrigida sits for Epstein

The Supreme Court of the USA had its moments of influence on the film industry when it overruled a ban by New York City State on the showing of the Italian *The Miracle*, (declaring that cities and states may not censor films on the grounds that they are sacrilegious) and by invalidating a ban by Marshall in Texas against *Pinky*, a film with strong racial connotations.

Mostly members of the audiences went to the cinema to be diverted and amused—not educated, and, for the time being audiences held up well despite the television challenge. Convenience had something to do with it, particularly in the USA where 'drive in' cinemas took the place of the many closed-down indoor theatres, their advantage lying in the convenience that the whole family could sit in the car and thus obviate the need for baby-sitters at home.

Television

Home convenience was, of course, the main attraction of television since it can hardly be claimed that the standard of programmes anywhere was very high. In Britain national coverage reached 80% that summer (the first European country to do so) though the number of hours viewing each day was limited to about five. In the week following the King's death programmes were in chaos but managed to recover in time to deliver an exemplary coverage of the funeral. As for the rest, standards were low, with music hall turns, parlour games, sport and circuses mixing uneasily with ballet and some rather pedantic news and current affairs programmes.

Dragnet and *I Love Lucy* were popular in the USA,

'I Love Lucy'

'What's my line?'

Below: *The first walkie-talkie television camera*

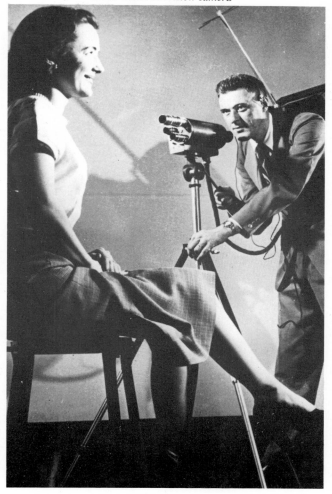

where the problems of an Administration ban (lifted in June) over constructing new transmitters had prevented the provision of complete coverage over a vast country. Programme quality was also to some extent exacerbated by viewing restrictions such as those imposed by colleges to limit football coverage, over the televising of House of Representative Committee sessions and agreements which forbade the televising of certain motion pictures until three years had elapsed since their first theatre showing. **Nevertheless US TV accomplished several important firsts**—nationwide coverage of the atomic tests, intensive showing of the Presidential Elections in all its stages and, on 7 June, the first public telecast of a major surgical operation from a Chicago hospital.

Advances in technology not only enhanced the quality of the picture but dramatically widened the scope of presentation. For example, 50 cinema theatres transmitted the **Walcott-Marciano fight** (see Section 6) live on 23 September on a wide screen, a method using the 625 line system similar to one being developed in Britain in 1951. The first steps towards the **integration of British and European transmissions** were demonstrated by an experiment in July, when programmes from the French 819 line System (the Louvre, a fashion show and sports) were converted to the British 405 line system in a cross-Channel link-up. It was hoped that, one day, standardisation in systems would be complete, for agreement was reached in 1952 to make the 625 system universal throughout Europe—an aspiration which has yet to be fulfilled completely. Ways to record television programmes on magnetic tape rather than on film were well advanced as well as progress made with **colour television** (which had previously been shown in the USA by CBS until they were stopped by the Administration on economy grounds). The prospects of improvements to outside broadcasts were helped by the use of a **'walkie-talkie'** camera with built-in power supply used at the Party Conventions in the USA.

The most important advance in **educational television**

was seen in Britain, where experimental programmes for schools began on 4 February, at a time when, for the first time in Britain, the sales of television sets were beginning to outstrip those of radios.

Broadcasting

From the angle of originality, 1952 was of only moderate interest for broadcast entertainment. Presentation techniques and coverage (no less than 98% of the population in the USA with 110 million sets and 67 million in Europe out of 249 million world-wide) remained at a peak of proficiency, which has changed little since, despite the challenge of television. In Britain two series of talks—one by **Arnold Toynbee** in the Reith Lectures on the subject of 'The World and the West' and the other by **Bertrand Russell** on 'Portraits from Memory', reached the intellectual peaks of the year. For the rest it was the mixture as before—of music, panel games, plays, variety shows such as *Take it From Here*, sports commentaries (with emphasis on the Olympic Games) and so on.

Political broadcasting centred upon propaganda battles between the Communist and Western worlds. While the USSR, China and their allies transmitted strongly to the

Arnold Toynbee

The 'Take It From Here' team. On the air Jimmy Edwards, Joy Nichols and Dick Bentley watched by Sally Rogers who would take over from Miss Nichols

The first detector van

uncommitted nations, who made little difficulty for those who wished to listen, the West, prompted by the USA and to a lessening effect by Britain (which reduced its overseas broadcasts on economy grounds) tried to break through intensive jamming by the Communists, who did not wish their people to hear voices from the rest of the world. The most notable project in this connection came from the USA which fitted out a freighter, *The Courier*, with three high-powered transmitters and positioned her in the Eastern Mediterranean to beam signals through the Iron Curtain and to the Middle East countries. Despite jamming and the general overcrowding of wavelengths, programmes continued to get through. Meanwhile, in the USA in May, greater freedom of listening was permitted when a judgement of the Supreme Court allowed broadcasts in public conveyances. In Britain the BBC's monopoly was extended for a further ten years, to the continued exclusion of commercial broadcasting, and the price of a sound licence (11 million) in Britain remained at £1 towards the £16 million spent on it annually. **The first use of detector** vans to uncover those who had not paid was announced as successful and due for more general application.

Music

Though the output of music through broadcasting, concerts and festivals reached a higher level and quality than ever before it cannot be said that much in the way of originality or lasting importance was introduced. To those brought up on traditional sounds and melodies the weird cacophonies of contemporary classical music were incomprehensible, though some, even of the philistines, drew pleasure from an entirely new instrument—an **electronic organ** made in the USA which used oscillators to generate sounds through loudspeakers.

Of the composers none of distinction made their mark in 1952, and of new classical compositions only one, **Ralph Vaughan Williams'** *Harmonica Concerto* was both successful and novel. With **Larry Adler** as the soloist it was often repeated, though 25 years later it is rarely heard.

Popular music filled the ether, the dance halls and the rooms of those who possessed a gramophone. **Pop Music Charts** of best sellers had first been seen in the *Billboard*

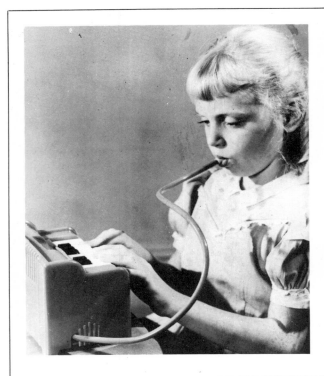

Above: *Mr and Mrs Larry Adler with the pianist Harriet Cohen* (*left*)

Left: *A toy organ made of plastic*

in the USA in 1936, but not until 14 November 1952 did the **first Top Ten Chart** appear in Britain for gramophone record sales. That chart clearly demonstrates the tone of the public's taste at the time:

1	*Here in my Heart*	**Al Martino**
2	*You belong to my Heart*	**Jo Stafford**
3	*Somewhere along the Way*	**Nat King Cole**
4	*Isle of Innisfree*	**Bing Crosby**
5	*Feet up*	**Guy Mitchell**
6	*Half as Much*	**Rosemary Clooney**
7	*High Noon*	**Frankie Laine**
	Forget-me-Not	**Vera Lynn**
8	*Sugar Bush*	**Doris Day** and **Frankie Laine**
	Blue Tango	**Ray Martin**
9	*Homing Waltz*	**Vera Lynn**
10	*Auf Wiedersehen*	**Vera Lynn**

Kiss of Fire and *Too Young* also did well in the USA. Strangely, however, the public turned away from singers such as **Johnny Ray** (who used to weep during his performances), in favour of healthily robust tenors like **Mario Lanza**. It was a time for straightforwardness, for melody and orthodox presentation for the masses.

The above chart is credited to the *Billboard*.

Mario Lanza

Vera Lynn

Bing Crosby

Opera, Ballet and Ballroom Dancing

The public preference in opera and ballet was much more catholic than with the rest of music. **Benjamin Britten**'s *Billy Budd*, **Alban Berg**'s *Wozzeck* and **George Gershwin**'s *Porgy and Bess* were well received in Britain (the former swiftly repeated in Paris) along with the usual repertoire of the established companies. At Salzburg, **Richard Strauss**'s *Lieber der Danae* received its first performance in a year made memorable by first performances of operas that, 25 years later, continue to be performed and recorded. Long-playing gramophone records (first introduced commercially in the USA in 1948) encouraged the sales of lengthy classical works such as opera and made far more people familiar and excited with entire works instead of, as until then, a few well-known and sometimes hackneyed themes.

Ballet, too, profited from the wider public knowledge made possible by earlier films and performances in the

Above: '*Billy Budd*'   Below: '*The Cage*'

John Field and Beryl Grey making a three-dimensional film

Jitterbugging

cinema and on television. Principally, however, this rapidly growing popularity was created by vastly improved standards of performance (notably in Britain) and the consolidation of a distinctive style formulated by the British Old Vic Company and, in the USA, (to a lesser extent) **Georges Balanchine**'s New York City Ballet. Balanchine's production of **Jerome Robbin**'s *The Cage* had done well in the USA and also in Paris, but in London received a cold shoulder. There they preferred such offerings as **Frederick Ashton**'s *Sylvia*, **John Cranko**'s *Bonne Bouche*, besides the traditional classical presentations. It said something for the immense strength of English Ballet that, in the absence of the great **Margot Fonteyn** (then in her early prime) and **Moira Shearer**, dancers of the calibre of the up-and-coming **Nadia Narina** and **Beryl Grey** could step lightly into their shoes in the most important parts to found international reputations that were to extend well into the future.

A spectacle well worth watching came from the **Dancers of Bali** who gave short seasons in Europe and the USA, and there were also visits from Indian dance companies and folk dancers from such countries as Yugoslavia. In effect, classical dancing rode the crest of a wave with far greater heights yet to ascend as it laid a strong ground swell for the future. For most people, however, dancing implied their own ballroom performance exemplified by the old established waltzes, fox-trots, played at social gatherings and in public halls. There the more complicated samba and the rumba encouraged simpler minds to concentrate on more complex steps while jitterbugging in its several forms expressed exuberance. The mood and scope was tempered for the most part by age and athletic agility.

Art

By the standards that are common enough 25 years later, the prices attained by paintings in the sale rooms of 1952, were low, almost stingy. Top price of the year seems to have gone to a small **Constable** oil of 1823—*Salisbury Cathedral from the Bishop's Garden*— sold at Christies's for 20 500 guineas. Nine impressions of **Goya**'s *Disasters of War* sold for £1800, but one of the surprise high prices of the year was £11 500 for **Bruegel**'s *Christ and the Woman taken in Adultery*. The modern painters were slightly out of favour. A **Renoir** landscape made but £460 and a small **Cézanne** oil was withdrawn when it failed to reach its reserve at £2940.

Public interest in art was strong, the Exhibition of **Leonardo da Vinci**'s works (on the 500th anniversary of his birth) at the Royal Academy being the outstanding event of the year. An exhibition in London of the work of **Pietro Annigoni** raised considerable interest, but it was French art which dominated the many exhibitions held throughout the world and the modern Impressionists who fetched the best sale prices in France. Among present-day painters **Graham Sutherland** was prominent, an exhibition of his work winning keen approval in Venice and Paris, while in the USA the first prize at the annual International Exhibition held by the Carnegie Institute was won for the first time by a Briton, **Ben Nicholson,** with his *5 December 1949*.

Taken in retrospect, and also by the standards of the time, 1952 was not a year for great or sensational movements from the world of art, recovering as it may have been from the convulsive activity of 1951 and the innovations of the Festival of Britain.

Annigoni at work

Literature

The number of titles published in Britain during 1952 was 18 741 (compared with about 16 000 in 1938 and over 30 000 25 years later). The USA produced only 8566. Britain, of course, was the dominant publishing country outside the ambit of the Russian Soviet bloc. Sheer weight of numbers did not reflect products of outstanding brilliance or quality in a year that failed to

Ernest Hemingway, the sea and the fish

see more than a handful of pre-eminent books. Biographies and memoirs sold best but not even **Harold Nicholson's** official biography of *King George the Fifth* was outstanding. Perhaps the most wide-ranging, best researched and best selling of all non-fiction works was **Chester Wilmot**'s *Struggle for Europe*, a large single volume history of the war in the West, rich in insight, which has well withstood the test of criticism and time. Another classic was **Ernest Hemingway**'s superb *The Old Man and the Sea* with its stirring and touching tale of an old man and a boy catching and trying to bring to shore a huge swordfish. The best seller fiction of the year in the USA was **Thomas Costain**'s *The Silver Chalice* with **Herman Wouk**'s *The Caine Mutiny*, the best seller of 1951, as runner up and also winner of the Pulitzer Prize. The great honour of Nobel Prize for Literature went that year to **François Mauriac** in recognition of his many achievements with the pen; he received £11 408. In France there appeared a short story by **Pierre Boulle** called *Le Pont de la rivière Kwai* that won him the **Sainte-Beuve Prize** for fiction but which, one day, was to make a far greater impact on the cinema screen. For the most part the well-known names predominated, each with his contribution of the year, while young writers, as usual, struggled for recognition with none that are now among the well-known breaking surface. Yet fresh material was being written in abundance and made to appear, with particular merit, by **John Lehmann**, with his *New Writing* and *New Sounds* anthologies that included poetry. Editors such as he, encouraged by publishers with the vision of **Allen Lane** (knighted in the New Year's Honours list and who had begun Penguin paperbacks in 1935 and spread them worldwide) along with support for numerous experimental—and successful—ventures, were vital to a future which, to some of the aspiring, looked rather drab.

From the statistics it appeared that people were reading more, the number of books lent from public libraries in Britain rising by about 7% in the year and a similar trend detectable elsewhere. **In Canada a National Library** was at last made possible by act of parliament, though its site had still to be chosen. Everywhere more libraries were being built at the same time as efforts were being made, notably in the USA, to acquire rare books and first editions. As a result the sharp increase in the price of old books was continued. An 1847 *Jane Eyre* fetched £240 and a 13th Century *Buxheim Psalter*, sold for £74 in 1932, raised £1350 in London to achieve what may have been the highest price made public that year.

François Mauriac

SECTION 5

THE ARENA OF DISCOVERY AND PROGRESS

Constructional Engineering

As the number of motor vehicles continued to increase, so too did the number and scope of grandiose major road building projects multiply, (see Section 3). The development of motorways was mainly held back by lack of funds (there were none as yet in Britain) but in Japan, for example, 325 miles were planned along with an ambitious scheme for an overhead ring road in Tokyo. By contrast, a country such as Ethiopia was so lacking in roads that, with US aid, it was forced to concentrate construction on 2500 secondary roads in addition to 5000 miles of primary ones. **Among the most spectacular road projects in the world** was the highway linking Caracas with La Guaraira in Venezuela which, along its $10\frac{1}{2}$ mile length through mountainous country, featured one of the longest cuttings in the world. One of its many bridges,

New roads in Caracas

nearing completion in 1952, was among the largest in the world and included a pre-stressed concrete span that was lifted into position in one piece. **The longest bridge and road project commenced in 1952** was 14 miles in length and was intended to link Tampa Bay, Florida, to Manatee County. In Brazil work started on a reinforced concrete arch bridge which, with its span of 610 ft, would be the third largest of its sort in the world.

The greater emphasis upon concrete structures as opposed to steel was, of course, stimulated by aggravating steel shortages. As a result much research and

without explaining for whom the others had been built. This type of 'utility' house would bring something new to British practice—a single living room with stairs rising out of it and heating performed by one boiler. More multi-storey blocks of flats were being built in Britain, a seven storey example at the new town of Stevenage attracting special attention because of its height alone. Undeniably this was the year in which, for the first time, the true post-war trend in architecture, which is taken for granted 25 years later, could readily

The Tampa Bay Bridge

development was promoted. A test which caught attention in Britain was the overloading to destruction of a pre-stressed concrete footbridge which had been built on the south bank of the River Thames for the Festival of Britain in 1951. Its 76 ft span, designed to carry a working load of 35 tons, was overloaded to 81 tons. At that point a failure took place that lead to an eventual, dramatic collapse of the entire span—a useful experiment because it served to prove the accuracy of the calculations that were made prior to construction.

There was a dire shortage of housing in almost every part of the world. In Britain, moreover, it was suggested that in most large towns '. . . the annual wastage exceeds the new accommodation made available'—and that at a time when **Mr Harold Macmillan** announced that over 200 000 houses would be completed in the ensuing year. Attempts were being made to limit the use of materials from between 5 and 10% in order to reduce costs by £150 each house. This was for a 'people's house'—

be discerned. Concrete was in common use along with a quite extensive employment of prefabricated sections. The names of **Sir Lewis Casson** in Britain (honoured for his work as Director of the Festival of Britain and as the architect in charge of the Van Riebeck Festival Fair in Capetown) and **Charles Le Corbusier** of France (a revolutionary celebrated for his **Unité d'Habitation** that was completed in Marseilles) were world famous.

Probably the most imaginative, and certainly the most ambitious, engineering project agreed upon in 1952 was the joint plan between the USA and Canada to construct the **St Lawrence Seaway** that, through a complex system of great locks and canals, would open up a route big enough for ocean going ships to sail from the Atlantic Ocean into the Great Lakes. By including the construction of associated hydro-electric plants, the task would take ten years. The completion of the 60 mile **Don Volga Canal** in Russia which linked these two rivers (and thereby the Baltic to the Black Sea) was an equally awe-inspiring achievement, hugely improving irrigation in addition to navigation, as it did, and acting as the first stage on what was to be a vast hydro-electric scheme.

Harold Macmillan and house

Le Corbusier's l'Unité d'Habitation

Communications

In the days before communication satellites had been seriously mooted, the commonest means of long-distance communication continued to be by land line or radio, mostly through land relay stations. In Britain it was claimed that by mounting the messenger boys on motorcycles, instead of pedal bicycles, 25% was knocked off the average time taken to deliver a telegram. Television, being restricted in transmission by its 'line-of-sight' characteristic, was thought to have another possibility when, in May, a notion was proposed in the USA that the ionosphere could reflect signals back to earth. However, the most important 'relinking' of 1952 was restoration of the cable (cut in wartime) between Britain and the USA, while the main project under consideration for a trans-Atlantic link was via 68 relay stations located on earth. A booming business in the USA was the service by Western Union in **transmitting facsimiles** by land line from place to place, department to department and desk to desk. Stores accounting was revolutionised,

Opening of the Don-Volga canal

A facsimile machine

banks could verify signatures at long range. Over 10 000 of these machines were said to have been in use in 1952 in 48 cities. And in Britain **Glyn Mills Bank was experimenting with closed circuit television** to scan bank accounts. Of much greater importance, however, was the addition, throughout the year, of telephonic links to some of the more isolated parts of the globe such as the Azores, Angola, Madagascar and Iraq.

As an expanding element in the world's communication systems, television was playing a much more significant part and, in this aspect, is dealt with more fully in Section 4. Here it is appropriate to mention the announcement in 1952 of the **world's first practical under-water, remotely controlled TV camera** which was developed in Britain. Not only had the problems of water proofing been successfully solved down to depths of 1200 ft, but ways to change and focus the lens, provide sufficient light (with a diver's lamp) and stabilise the body with a fin had been settled. Its first practical use came in locating and identifying the submarine HMS *Affray* which had sunk in mysterious circumstances in the Channel in 1951.

Above: *Glyn Mills closed circuit television*   Below: *Television from under the sea*

Turbine Engines

The dominant position of Britain in the design and manufacture of gas-turbine engines has been touched upon in Section 3. In 1952 the **Bristol Company** announced the most powerful jet engine yet, the Olympus with a thrust of 9750 lb at sea level and which was almost at once taken under licence by the **Wright Co** in the the USA for manufacture there as the J 67. At the other end of the scale was the little **Ruston and Hornsby 750 Kv gas-turbine generator** which completed 3000 hours running (700 non-stop in one period) with few snags to become the first British production engine of the kind besides the first to run on dried peat. The value of such a generator in a country like Ireland, where it could be sited in a remote area adjacent to its fuel supply, could hardly be underrated, besides its great economy of action in quick starting for use at times of sudden peak demand. Intensive research lead to continuing improvements to jet engines, particularly on materials or processes to enhance the production, performance and life of the vital turbine blades. New machining methods cut production costs; special coatings added life; and the new nickel chromium alloy called **Nimonic 95** was found to give a better performance than its predecessor.

The Ruston and Hornsby 750 Kv gas-turbine generator

Interesting Patents applied for

The synchro-cyclotron, a very powerful atom-smasher.
A means of **relaying television pictures** over long distances via high flying aircraft.

A way of **transmitting colour pictures** by land line or radio.
Several new **titanium alloys**.
A typewriter in Chinese characters.
A way of **turning coal into oil** while still underground.
The **sterilisation of raw canned foods** by high-frequency radio waves.

Science and Medicine

Ironically two of the most important pieces of medical research appeared, on the face of it, somewhat contradictory. On the one hand there were the scientists who discovered more potent ways of animal fertilisation, and on the other hand those who tried out a way to prevent it in humans. The **artificial insemination of cattle** began early in the 1940s in the USA, but in 1952 a paper published at Cambridge University proposed ways of greatly multiplying the method by deep-freezing the semen so that it could be preserved and transported over long distances. By this means one bull could be 'mated' with thousands of cows instead of the then average of 50. Moreover it meant that, by selective control (later with the aid of memory stored computors), the rate of improved breeding could be speeded up and new strains produced. As a trial, semen from a British bull was successfully used in cows in South Africa. This process is now, of course, commonplace and very beneficial by increasing meat and milk supplies through the improvement of stock.

In the USA a controlled experiment was begun, using 300 human couples, to study the behaviour of the **first oral contraceptive—the Pill**—which was made of phosphorylated hesperidin and taken once daily. The tests were intended to last over a number of years. In parallel

The Pope and the people

would arise the religious counter reaction stimulated by the Pope's declaration in 1951 that 'so called birth control methods were incompatible with the law of God'. In 1952, when the World Health Organisation tried to promote a Norwegian proposal that backward nations should be advised on birth control, the debate had to be abandoned because the Roman Catholic countries threatened a walk-out.

An accusation by the Russians in March that the Americans had initiated **biological warfare** in Korea by dropping specimens from the air, refocused public attention upon a type of warfare which in one form or another had recurred for centuries. Although photographs of the offending species were eventually produced by the Chinese, the request by the USA that international inspection should be carried out in order to refute the accusations was repeatedly prevented. The matter hit the headlines, as it was intended to do, motion and counter motion were floated through the United Nations and mass protest demonstrations at appropriate moments were arranged within Communist countries until the whole matter died away from lack of indignant interest.

Nevertheless, the prospect of anything sensational in the way of health remedies was usually assured of headline treatment. The so-called wonder drug **Cortizone** was first manufactured in 1952 (having been discovered in 1949), but quite soon it was realised that it only gave relief and did not provide the cure for rheumatism that

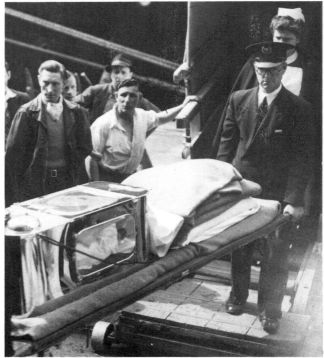

An oxygen tent

had been hoped. Likewise pronounced doubts came to be expressed about **antibiotics**, the celebrated penicillin, streptomycin and terramycin drugs (to name but three) and to which **erythromycin** and **carbomycin** were added in 1952. It had been found that the human body began gradually to build up resistance to the antibiotics to such an extent that an article in the *British Medical Journal* forecast that penicillin was 'a wasting asset'. This realisation merely stimulated even more intensive research, particularly since it was observed that people were taking the new drugs in such quantity that wholesale resistance *was* possible.

Televising a dental operation

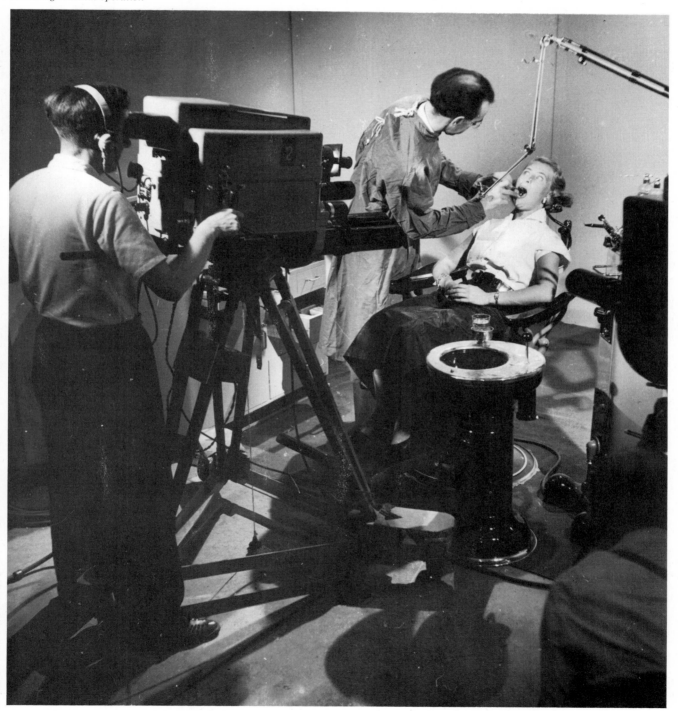

Another 'wonder' of science that took great steps forward was the **radio isotope** in commercial form. First named as such in 1913, and recognised in the years following as having a part to play in scientific research, medicine and industry, they became 'big-business' for Britain when, in 1952, she emerged, with 4000 consignments, as the world's chief exporter. World-wide, however, highly intensive investigation was being made into the whole subject of radiation, a continuous activity that was to revolutionise scientific knowledge in the years to come.

An important outcome of scientific investigation and the more general interest and understanding of its meaning by people at large, was an increasing awareness of the ecological problems that needed a solution. An ecological and economic problem which had worried agriculturalists for generations was the proliferation of the rabbit. Attempts to introduce the **myxoma virus** (which at one time was found only in the Brazilian wild rabbit), and cause disease among Australian rabbits so to reduce their numbers, had failed on several occasions prior to 1950, when at last it caught hold. By the end of 1952, 85% of the rabbits of southeastern Australia had been wiped out. As an experiment in June 1952, the same virus was introduced into France by **A Delille** among rabbits on his land near Paris and with such effect that, within a few months, an almost total extermination had taken place. Moreover the disease spread, leaving in its wake millions of rabbits which, as they perished, displayed the horribly unpleasant signs of deterioration which were characteristic of the disease's effect. Counter measures instituted by the French could not arrest the spread of **myxomatosis**: soon it would spread all over Europe and, in places, produce a death rate that could be as high as 99.8%.

Rabbit, still alive, with myxomatosis

Gentler investigations revealed there was a distinct relation between the study of homing characteristics in birds to the protection of migratory flocks. The performance of a **Manx Shearwater**, which was taken from South Wales to Boston, USA, and flew home the 2800 nautical miles in 12¾ days, seemed all the more remarkable when it was pointed out that the Shearwater does not fly in a straight line, never visits North America and

A Shearwater

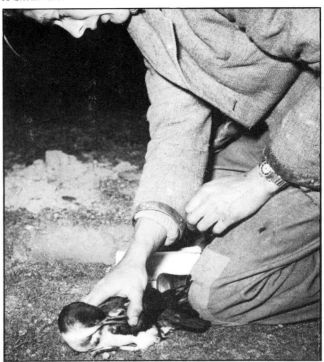

would probably spend from 2 to 6 hours a day resting and feeding. Therefore it must have flown on a precisely sensed bearing at an average speed of about 20 mph following a course of which it had no previous knowledge. **A nationwide survey of sea birds** (lasting for six months until 31 March) by the British Royal Society for the Protection of Birds and its associates produced the alarming news that 50 000 to 250 000 sea birds amounting to 54 species had been affected by oil pollution from tankers that winter, and that this threat to bird life was one which would undoubtedly multiply to really dangerous levels as the world turned more and more to oil as a fuel.

A man who had ample opportunity to examine the condition of the ocean ecology was the French scientist **Dr Alain Bombard**. In a carefully planned experiment, prompted by knowledge of the innumerable fatal cases among wartime sailors who had been cast adrift after their ships had been sunk, he set out to prove that man on his own could survive at sea by living off the liquid contained in fish, off fish meat and also plankton. Starting on 11 August in his rubber raft called '*L'Hérétique*,' he was 65 days at sea, catching his provisions in a fine mesh scoop before arriving in good shape at Barbados on Christmas Eve. Indeed, it was his opinion that physical survival was the lesser problem: the demands of solitude placed a far heavier tax upon morale, he said.

Alain Bombard and his rubber boat

Senator Pat McCarran (right)

The morale of the scientific world was certainly deeply disturbed in 1952. In Britain in September the address by the President of the British Association (**Professor A V Hill**) at its annual gathering took as its subject 'The Ethical Dilemma of Science'. Professor Hill posed questions which searched deeply into the demands placed upon scientists: for example, the relationship between those whose efforts aimed to produce more food, and others who were causing a population explosion by helping people stay alive longer; the dangers to the environment inherent in certain new insecticides such as DDT; the irony of excellent communication systems being employed to disseminate lies and disorder; above all, the scientists' responsibility in making war easier to start and then immeasurably more destructive. In the shadow of the hydrogen bomb and tales of germ warfare, these questions aroused widespread concern and were a frequent subject for discussion among worried people. On the other side of the Atlantic the problem could be seen from yet another angle in that the **1950 McCarran Act on Security** and the **1952 Act on Immigration** (both of which had been vetoed by President Truman and re-established by a Republican majority in Congress, and were later to be heavily amended as unconstitutional by the Supreme Court) were preventing the free movement of scientists and also the interchange of scientific information. Scientific meetings which had been planned to take place in the USA had to be held elsewhere and prominent American citizens who spoke out against this tight security stood the chance of being pilloried in public by **Senator Joseph McCarthy** and his virulent committee investigating un-American activities (see Section 2).

Another classic subject for debate also centred upon the USA (though it was equally liable to occur in any other civilised country) concerned **the use of animals for scientific experiment**. The New York State Legislature enacted a measure which permitted homeless dogs and cats to be used for medical research. This threw pet owners, fearing for their loved ones' safety, into close league with anti-vivisectionists against the scientists who successfully argued that human beings depended upon experiments upon animals for the protection of their own health.

Not in the least bit controversial (because they dealt with precise scientific facts) were the remarkable archaeological discoveries made possible by the practical utilisation of **radiocarbon dating**. This technique had been known prior to 1950, but it was in 1952 that the results then actually achieved aroused great excitement. It was then, for example, that man-made objects in America were dated at 8000 BC, even older than the walls of Jericho which, until 1952, were thought to date back to 3000 BC but which, under investigation by the British **Dr Kathleen Kenyon**, were found to belong to 7000 BC.

Discoveries large and small

The search for fresh knowledge about things ancient, as well as delvings into those areas that lay beyond the frontiers of all previous knowledge, grew in pace as the recovery from the Second World War became more assured and greater resources could be switched to that sort of activity. In the realms of archaeological research the most interest in 1952 focused upon discoveries made in connection with the ancient sites of the Aegian Civilisation and, particularly, in respect of the **Cemetry of Chamber Tombs at Knossos**. These had been found in 1950, and in 1951 were described by **M Hood** at the annual meeting of the British School of Architecture, at which mention was also made of many magnificent finds of weapons and armour. And yet the crucial revelation in relation to this bronze age civilisation was yet to be announced: **Michael Ventris** and **J Chadwick** were on the verge of completing the deciphering of the so-called **Linear B Script** which had first been discovered on clay tablets at Knossos at the beginning of the century. At **Mycenae**, too, new tombs dating from 1600 BC (the same period as the Knossos civilisation) were discovered and with them fresh hope that the legendary stories of Homer could be established as fact. Here were found, by **A Wace** and **L Papadimitrion**, burial relics including what was supposed to be Clytemnestra's grave, the 'house of the wine merchant' and the 'house of the oil merchant', a painting of a warrior on horseback and many tablets inscribed with the Linear B script.

At **Lullingstone** in Kent, the discovery was made of the first archaeological evidence of Christianity in Britain, plaster fragments from the wall of a Roman

Exhibits at Knossos

building with paintings of saintly and religious figures. These appear to date from the 3rd century. On the same site **Lt-Col G W Mears**, the director of excavations, found a number of other interesting items such as agricultural buildings and apparatus, coins and, imprinted into a stone base, the footprints of a dog which must have run across when the mortar was still wet.

Roman mosaics at Lullingstone

The Mountains of the Moon

Exploratory expeditions in 1952 took many directions. **Professor W Q Kennedy** went with a geological party to the supposed **Mountains of the Moon** of the geographer Ptolemy at the southern end of the Ruwenzori Range bordering Uganda and the Belgian Congo (Zaire)—a part of the world which 'had never before been seen by human eyes'. Probably the claim was a little far fetched since the area was populated by natives and there had been a series of expeditions to the region from other nations throughout the previous 50 years. Even so there was justification in calling this territory 'the most remarkable landscape in the world', for it encompassed 40 square miles of 40 to 50 volcanic craters, some $2\frac{1}{2}$ miles in diameter and 650 ft deep in a region that was said to be teeming with wild life, from elephants to buck, kites to warblers.

Return of the Swiss expedition to Everest

The return in February, after just over two years' absence in the Antarctica, of members of the first international polar expedition in history (an Anglo–Norwegian–Swedish venture) underlined the increasing interest of several nations in this barren part of the world. At the same time four separate expeditions were beginning to penetrate the Himalayas, three of them with the intention of placing the first man on the summit of **Mount Everest.** On 28 May a Swiss team led by **Dr Edouard Wyss-Dunant** and including **Sherpa Tensing,** reached 28 215 ft. On 22 November another Swiss expedition, which also included Tensing, but this time led by **Dr Gabriel Chevalley,** failed on the South Col. Oxygen apparatus was used during the spring assault, though it had proved somewhat ineffective above 27 500 ft due to a technical inadequacy. Nevertheless, there were those who prognosticated that, for physiological reasons, the summit would never be reached. Meanwhile a British team led by **Eric Shipton** had explored the south-west of the mountain and at one point reached an altitude of 27 790 ft. Little publicised at the time, but apparently operating simultaneously with the second Swiss expedition, there seems also to have been a Russian team trying to reach the peak of Everest. This expedition, from the evidence of Polish sources, seems to have figured in the **worst mountaineering disaster** in history with the loss of 40 lives.

Further interest in Everest was generated by the Swiss who brought back photographs of footprints thought to be made by a four-footed animal weighing, it was suggested, 150 lb, thus giving further credence to the myth of the **Abominable Snowman**—a subject which, 25 years later, remains a myth.

Descending rather than climbing upwards, and assuming a genuine scientific desire to discover the point at which an underground river, running through deep caves in the Pyrenees came into the open, a Belgian expedition led by **Professor Max Cosyns** entered the depths with a view to going below the 1510 ft level reached in the same caves in 1951. Unfortunately the leading pot-holer, **Marcel Loubens,** was the victim of a fault in his equipment and fell 1200 ft to his death. An enormous cavern, 1600 ft long, 1000 ft wide and 400 ft high was, nevertheless, found while colouring thrown into the river eventually reappeared 4 miles away and 3000 ft further down, suggesting that here was a vast potential source for hydro-electric power, a suggestion which has yet to be exploited on a large scale.

The greatest depth explored by man was from the British Survey Ship *Challenger* which returned home in

Scientists from the Challenger *with instruments and specimen*

September 1952 after a 2½ year circumnavigation of the world. She had taken soundings in the Mariannas Trench, Pacific Ocean, in 1951 at the greatest depth ever, 5960 fathoms (35 710 ft and thus much farther below sea level than Everest's peak is above). Additionally, she had brought up water samples from 5594 fathoms and had discovered a 7000 ft 'high' mountain 400 miles to the west of Cape St Vincent in the Atlantic. In the same period the Danish Deep Sea Expedition in the **Galathea** had found living organisms at 34 000 ft below sea level— some 9000 ft below the level which, until then, had been supposed possible. In October a French expedition set sail on a four year voyage which, in time to come, was to provide a rich store of information about ocean life as well as giving endless pleasure to the millions of people who watched the film produced on television and in cinemas. This was **Capitaine Jacques Cousteau**'s 350 ton ship *Calypso*, equipped with the most modern diving facilities and the benefit of experience he had gained in the previous decade.

In quite the opposite direction of search lay the investigations into **Space and the Universe**—that half-serious subject, as it was mockingly called. The revolutionary new theory which had been thrown into the debate in 1948 by the Cambridge astronomers, **H Bondi**

Jacques Cousteau

Contemporary artist's impression of a moon rocket

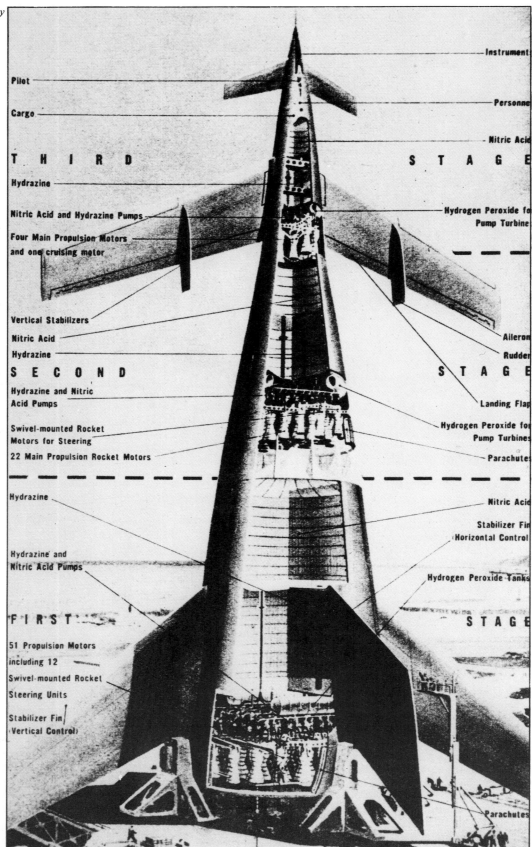

Pilot

Cargo

THIRD

Hydrazine

Nitric Acid and Hydrazine Pumps

Four Main Propulsion Motors and one cruising motor

Vertical Stabilizers

Nitric Acid

Hydrazine

SECOND

Hydrazine and Nitric Acid Pumps

Swivel-mounted Rocket Motors for Steering

22 Main Propulsion Rocket Motors

Hydrazine

Hydrazine and Nitric Acid Pumps

FIRST

51 Propulsion Motors including 12 Swivel-mounted Rocket Steering Units

Stabilizer Fin Vertical Control

Instrument

Personne

Nitric Acid

STAGE

Hydrogen Peroxide fo Pump Turbine

Aileron

Rudder

STAGE

Landing Flap

Hydrogen Peroxide fo Pump Turbines

Parachute

Nitric Acid

Stabilizer Fin Horizontal Control

Hydrogen Peroxide Tanks

STAGE

Parachutes

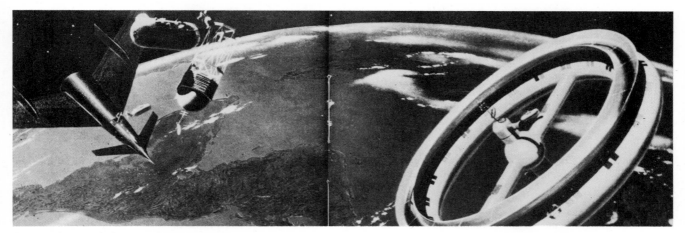

Space junk of the future, as visualised in 1952

and **T Gold**, that the universe was in a constant state of expansion, was under critical investigation. With **Fred Hoyle** they propounded a theory of 'steady state cosmology', which claimed that new matter was being continuously created from nothing throughout intergalactic space. This theory has since been seriously challenged but in 1952, it was at the centre of many learned discussions in gatherings such as those of the British Royal Institution. Moving a little closer home, Mr Hoyle wrote in the *Times* in October that, although interplanetary travel was feasible using rocket propelled vehicles, a great many problems had yet to be overcome, including those of avoiding fast-moving particles in space. He rejected the possibility of travel outside the solar system but thought that man might go to and from the Moon within the next 100 years. Quite unabashed by this, **G V Thompson** had produced estimates at the International Aeronautical Conference in Stuttgart by which he calculated the future use of 1000 tons of fuel at a time for a daily journey to the moon at a total cost of some $100 to 200 million per annum, or as much as $400 million if liquid hydrogen was used.

Much more down to earth were the predictions of **S F Singer** of the USA when he spoke of using rockets to place 'solar observatories' in orbit round the Earth to act as stations from which information about atomic particles from the Sun, ultra-violet rays and much more data besides could be gathered. Also these orbiting vehicles, which might in due course re-enter the Earth's atmosphere and be destroyed, could serve as relay stations for radio signals. This Singer foresaw taking place within the next few years.

Much of the new information available to astronomers came from the many new instruments, particularly those of the radio kind, being made available. In 1952 work was being pushed ahead on even more powerful steerable radio telescopes, notably at Jodrell Bank in England (to supplement the existing 'fixed' model), and at Ohio University in the USA. On 25 February, for the first time, a total eclipse of the sun was observed by both optical and radio means—a team of astronomers in the Sudan making the best of a clear sky to obtain good results. Although the results from this event would be long in gestation before publication, they would merely add to a

vast accumulation of information then becoming known from other sources. For example, the Mount Palomar observatory in the USA, with its great 200-inch telescope, told of amazing photographs of the Milky Way which, it now suggested, contained over 200 million stars. Moreover, it was becoming plain that the universe was filled with many millions more of unknown bodies, in

The 200-inch telescope at Mount Palomar, California

thousands of nebulae, and that astronomers of the future would be quite over-burdened by the work which their analysis would demand.

The **planet Jupiter** yielded fresh information in 1952 from the results of an examination by **N Nicholson** of photographs taken through the Mount Wilson 60 inch and 100 inch telescopes in 1951. For the first time it was seen that there was a twelfth satellite, the smallest of them all, with a diameter of 14 miles (compared with 3120 miles for the largest) that orbited about 13 million miles from the planet itself. At about the same time, **W Baum** and **A Code** were able to determine the concentration of molecules on Jupiter by observing the occulation of a star in relation to the atmosphere of the planet.

Probably the most dramatic astronomic discovery announced in 1952 was that of **Galactic Spiral Arms**, (first found in 1951 by **W Morgan** and his collaborators) of Orion, Perseus and Sagittarius. With the knowledge of the existence of 'radio stars' in at least 50 areas where stars had never been found before, it dawned upon the world that the universe contained mysteries that were vastly more complex than had ever entered their dreams. Few people could imagine the results from this discovery even when it was suggested, for example, that the manifestations of radio stars might affect television as well as radar in the same way as sunspots affected them.

Some idea of the practical everyday importance of astronomy was provided in reverse, by the neutralisation of the **Mount Stromko Observatory, Australia,** by a disastrous fire in February. Not only was valuable equipment destroyed that had taken ten years to collect and was valued at £80 000, but the elimination of power denied ships at sea a time service for navigational purposes, until they could tune into Greenwich Observatory from the Equator.

A Galactic spiral Nebula

Probably the most prolific field for discovery lay in the realms of **botany and zoology**. It came not only from expeditions such as that from Sydney, Australia,

which began searching in remote areas of north-west Australia, and in June, found a myriad of new plants, insects and animals. New species of plants, previously unknown in Britain, were still being discovered, too, while in the Scilly Isles **Miss Hilda Quick** recorded the sighting of an iridescent green bird about the size of a cuckoo, with a long bill. This turned out to be the first time the blue-checked bee-eater had been seen in Britain. The published results of an earlier assessment by the US National Museum went to show that, every year, zoologists were finding vast numbers of new species—5000 insects, 500 molluscs, up to 30 new mammals and even a few birds. For example, a whole new range of life previously left alone had been brought, literally, to the surface by a trawl from the Danish ship *Galathea* (mentioned above). From depths below 21 000 ft in the North Pacific many anemones, echinoderms, bivalves and marine worms had been dredged up. The leader of this expedition, **Dr Anton Brunn**, went so far as to claim that, although he had found no evidence of sea serpents, he fully believed that such things, in the form of giant eels, did exist.

As proof of assertions that supposedly extinct life still existed came the sensational rediscovery in December of the **Coelacanth**—a fish which, it had been assumed until 1938 from fossil remains and lack of a living species, had disappeared 70 million years before. This capture had been described as the most interesting and important find of this century and was made off the east coast of South Africa. Unfortunately only the skin and the skull of the 1938 specimen was retained and so it was a moment for great excitement when, 14 years later, a second coelacanth was brought to the surface alive—a 5 ft fish weighing 120 lb, coloured bright, steel-blue with dark blue eyes and three sets of fins remarkably like stunted arms and legs—a creature which had existed 350 million years ago and had once abounded upon earth. Fortunately the native fishermen who had found it off Madagascar had brought it to an English sea captain who possessed sufficient formalin to effect preservation. Great publicity was generated when **Professor J L B Smith**, of Rhodes University College, appealed to Dr Malan, the South African Prime Minister, for help in taking him to the island to study the fish. In gratitude he named the fish **Malania ajouanae** under the misapprehension that this was a new species—and so the story stood at the end of 1952. Subsequently, however, Professor Smith was to learn that the coelacanth was quite

Coelacanth

well known to the local fishermen who were accustomed to using its tough scales to roughen the inner tubes of their bicycles when repairing punctures. Furthermore, within less than a year, yet another one had been caught and today there are over a score to be seen in various museums. None of this, of course, belittles the discovery of what amounts to a genuine missing link with the distant past.

Prize Winners in Science

In 1952 fell the centenary of the year of birth of six previous winners of **Scientific Nobel Prizes**—Emil Fischer, chemist; Albert Michelson, physicist; Henry Moissan, chemist; Antoine Becquerel, physicist; William Ramsay, chemist; and Jacobus Van't Hoff, chemist. The same year itself produced the names of five men distinguished in science of whom three made important contributions to medicine. But as an echo of the past were the awards made in Britain to those whose inventions had produced vital weapons in the Second World War, particularly the £50 000 given to **Sir Robert Watson-Watt** who had been the first in Britain to propose the use of radio waves to locate aircraft at long range—the origination of research that led to the rapid development of radar, along with exploitation of the cathode ray tube to 'floodlight' the sky with radio waves.

The 1952 Nobel Prize for Physics was awarded jointly to two Americans who had worked concurrently (without knowledge of each other's project) on the discovery of nuclear magnetic resonance in solids—work which was fundamental to future developments in the field of physics. The men concerned were **Felix Bloch**, a naturalised Swiss whose initial education took place in Zürich, but whose research into magnetic movements, radar and nuclear induction was undertaken at Stamford University, California, and **Edward Purcell**. Purcell worked at Harvard and in 1952, besides receiving his share of the Nobel Prize, achieved something that was probably more important even than his previous work—the detection in collaboration with **Harold Ewen** of the **21 cm line**, a discovery which disclosed the distribution of hydrogen in galaxies and thus put radio astronomy (mentioned above) on a completely new footing.

The Nobel Prize for Chemistry was also jointly awarded to two Britons, but in this instance for a team effort between **Archer Martin** and **Richard Synge**. They had succeeded in identifying and separating chemical elements by chromatography, a relatively simple analytical method (far superior to intricate chemical processes) with many applications in industry, biology, medicine and the analysis of air pollution, oils and food products.

Selman Waksman, an American born in the Ukraine, the winner of the Nobel Prize in Physiology and Medecine, received his award for a discovery that had far more popular appeal than the subjects of his colleagues in other departments of science: he was the 'creator' in 1944 of **Streptomycin**, the first effective antibiotic in the treatment of different types of tubercular infections—a compound which has since revealed its limitations, due

Sir Robert Watson-Watt

Selman Waksman

to certain dangerous effects it can produce, such as paralysis, and various inhibitions to its application. However, it still has an important role to play in medical treatment.

Among the medals presented by The Royal Society of Britain was one to **Sir Frederick Bartlett**, an expert in animal behaviour, for his founding at Cambridge of a school for psychological behaviour. In America the Daniel Guggenheim medal was given to a Briton, **Sir Geoffrey De Havilland**, for 'forty years of pioneering in military and commercial aircraft'—a very appropriate award in the year of the DH Comet (see above). In America, too, development of work on that most important enthralling aspect of aviation, the quest for supersonic speeds, was recognised by the award of the **Collier Trophy** (established in 1911) to **John Stack** for his efforts in developing a transonic wind tunnel, the presentation being made by President Truman, on behalf of the National Aeronautical Association. To maintain proportion, however, it is perhaps worth concluding this section with the information that, while each Nobel Prize was valued at $32 910, the **Pillsbury Award for Domestic Science** made to **Mrs Harlib** of Chicago for a recipe for cookies netted her $25 000, plus a General Electric Kitchen.

SECTION 6

SPORTS
AND GAMES

The dominating sporting event of the year had to be the Olympic Games although their impact on public imagination in 1952 was less then than it is 25 years later, since in those days the news media did not saturate their audience to the same extent. For sheer drama, sound broadcasting could not compete with television but television in 1952 could not send live pictures direct to the rest of the world from Norway or Finland. The Games are mentioned in Section 1 and also below. The remainder of the Sporting Calendar followed its routine course by producing the customary exciting finishes, dramatic wins and tragic failures along with a respectable crop of records.

The Olympic Stadium, Helsinki

Athletics

The outstanding personality of the year was **Emil Zatopek** (Czechoslovakia), who won three Olympic Gold medals (5 and 10 000 metres plus the Marathon, all in Olympic record time) and also, during the year, took the World's Records for 15 miles, 25 and 30 km. Australian women produced some remarkable per-

Marjorie Jackson training for the Olympics

formances in the sprints, with **Marjorie Jackson** taking Gold Medals in the 100 and 200 metres events (the latter with a world record time) and **Shirley Strickland** doing the same in the 80 metres hurdles, also with a world record time. Seventeen Gold Medals went to men athletes from the USA while Soviet Russia took only two, won by women in the weight putting and discus throwing. Britons failed badly on the Olympic track although, prior to the Games, **Jim Peters** had run the fastest time ever for the Marathon distance (42 km) in 2 hours 20 minutes 42.2 seconds.

Badminton

For the second time in its history the Thomas Cup (founded in 1948) went to **Malaya** when the United States failed in their challenge by 7–2 matches. Malaya's dominance of the game rested on the prowess of the brothers **Choong**, and **Wong Peng Soon**, but already the Danish threat, in this increasingly popular game, was on the horizon. Having despatched the British 9–0, the Danes went down 3–6 to India who were in turn beaten 5–4 by the USA. Also Denmark produced the All-England Women's Champion in **Mrs Tommy Ahm**.

Baseball

Stan Musial

The **New York Yankees** persisted in their winning ways in taking the World Series by defeating the **Brooklyn Dodgers** in a great series, by 4–3, and thus equalling their previous record (1936–9) of four consecutive wins. It was also a series in which no less than 44 records were broken and 16 tied, with the Yankees (who also were top of the league) gaining a preponderant share of them. Two batters, **Paul Waner** (Pittsburg Pirates) and **Harry Heilmann** (Detroit Tigers) were elected to the Hall of Fame and the great **Stan Musial** (St Louis Cardinals) topped the National League batting with a .336 average. In the All-Star Game the National League defeated the American League 3–2 before a crowd of 32 785, who saw **Bobby Shantz** (Philadelphia Athletes) strike out the three men to whom he pitched. Top of the National League in Pitching was **Connelly** (New York Yankees) with 1.00% from only 11 games, whereas **Yuhas** (St. Louis Cardinals) was second with .857 from 54 games.

Basketball

This sport continued its steady progress, mostly in the USA, both through a rapidly improving standard of play as well as the steady sophistication of its rules. In the USA the professional game had a stronghold (the new men's champions for 1951–2 being the **Minneapolis Lakers**) and the Olympic title also went, as it always had done, to the USA who defeated the USSR 36–25. The women's game maintained its amateur status with **Baskin High School** proceeding steadily from the start it had made in 1947 to a record of 218 consecutive wins, to be completed in 1953. Unhappily the year was marred by the sentences on a few individuals for past misdemeanours in 'fixing' professional men's games. A New York judge hit at commercialism in basketball and football and cited the **University of Kentucky**. Two 'fixers' were sent to prison.

Harlem Globetrotters versus Boston Whirlwinds

Willie Mosconi

Billiards and Snooker

Willie Mosconi (USA) remained the pocket billiards champion, a position he had acquired in 1941 and held with only three interruptions since. However, the amateur game at last saw a change in its champion, with **Leslie Driffield** (Britain) supplanting **Robert Marshall** (Australia) who had held the title since 1936. Another Australian of great renown, **Walter Lindrum**, chalked up what remains the world's fastest (unofficial) billiards century break on 10 October in 27.5 seconds. In the USA **Willie Hoppe** retired at the end of an era which had begun in 1906 by winning his 51st 'world' championship in the US variant of the game.

At Snooker the World's Professional Championship went to **Fred Davis** (Britain).

Boxing

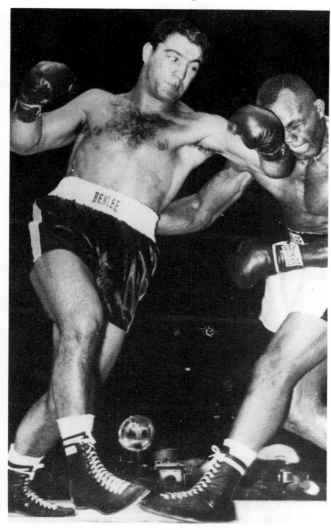

The Marciano punch which defeated Joe Walcott

The most sensational professional fight of the year was between the great **'Sugar' Ray Robinson**, (USA) world middle-weight title holder and **Joey Maxim** (USA), light heavy-weight champion for the latter's title. In a 104°F heatwave in New York on 25 June, Robinson was in sight of victory at the end of the 13th round, but heat exhaustion prevented him from leaving his corner for the 14th and so he lost by a technical knock-out. A thoroughly bruising contest was always in prospect when **Rocky Marciano** (USA) took the ring and this was his year for the heavy-weight title. A 'fighter', he defeated **Lee Savold** (USA) in the 7th round in February, **Bernie Reynolds** (USA) in the 3rd in May, **Harry Matthews** in the 2nd in July and went on in September to take the title from **Jersey Joe Walcott** in the 13th on 23 September by a knockout. At the time it was thought he would remain

champion for some time, as was to prove correct. Yet, in a year when few debuts of note were made, a young man called **Floyd Patterson** (USA) won the middle-weight title at the Olympic Games to lay the foundations of a career that was to be as distinguished as Marciano's Indeed, the USA dominated world boxing both in the amateur and professional ring. Five out of the ten Olympic titles went her way and five out of the eight world professional titles were hers, only the welter-weight belonging to **Kid Gavilan** (Cuba), the bantam-weight to **Jimmy Carruthers** (Australia) and the fly-weight to **Yoshio Sharai** (Japan). British boxing was in the doldrums with **Randolph Turpin** the only likely contender for a world title.

Chess

Mikhail Botvinnik (Russia) remained world champion at the peak of his form in a game which continued to be dominated by both Russian men and women. In the zonal final tournament in Stockholm the first four places were taken by Russians, with **A Kotov** first, and another Russian sharing fifth place with three others. **E Bikova** (Russia) won the women's world championship at Moscow.

Cricket

This was a year of debacles with the West Indies losing 4–1 in the Test Matches in Australia, and the Indians losing three and drawing one Test against England in England, their final defeat at Old Trafford being by an innings and 207 runs. Surrey won the English County Championship to begin an epoch of triumph, as they could scarcely fail to do with a team that included **Alec Bedser, Tony Lock, Jim Laker, Peter May** and several more who were playing or would play one day for England. Top of the English batting averages at 64.62 was **David Sheppard** (Sussex) (25 years later a Bishop) and top of the bowling an aggressive young Yorkshireman called **Fred Truman** with 61 wickets for 13.78 a piece. A young batsman called **Colin Cowdrey** was making a big impression for Oxford, and **Garfield Sobers** made his debut for the West Indies. Of the old guard, **Len Hutton** captained England and batted as well as ever (he was third in the averages behind Sheppard and May) and **Lindsay Hassett** led Australia brilliantly.

Cycling

Italians held pride of place through the powers of **Enzo Sacchi**, who took the World's Amateur Sprint title in Paris in August, **Fausto Coppi**, who won both the Tour of France and of Italy, and **P Fornara** who won the Tour of Switzerland. In the USA **Andy Blackman** won the 62½ mile Grand Prix of Long Island, while the World Professional Road Championship over 173.92 miles was won by **Heinz Müller**, the amateur race going to another Italian, **Luicano Ciancola**.

Outstanding among women cyclist was **Eileen Sheridan**

Eileen Sheridan

(Britain) who, within the year, broke five track and ten road records, the latter including a journey of 16 hours 45 minutes 47 seconds from Land's End to London.

Fencing

World Championships were not held in the Olympics year and so mention for this sport was focused on events at Helsinki, where the brilliant **Christian d'Oriola (France)** won the individual foil and helped France to win the Team foil event by remaining undefeated. Likewise **Edoardo Mangiarotti (Italy)** won the individual epée while his country won the team event and **Pál Kovacs (Hungary)** the sabre champion, helped his country to defeat Italy in the team event. There was a tie (5 wins each) for the women's gold in the foil between a past champion, **Ilona Elek (Hungary)**, and **Irene Camber (Italy)** that was decided by one hit.

Football (Association)

In a year that was unremarkable on the field, except in the English Cup Final, a lot of attention was focused on an investigation into the professional game as a result of which it was recommended that no transfer fee should be in excess of £15 000, one third to go to the Football League, one third to the players benevolent fund and the other third to the club. **Manchester United** were top of the British Division 1, **Hibernians** top of the Scottish Division A, **Motherwell** beat **Dundee** 4–0 in the Scottish Cup before 136 294 people, and 100 000 saw **Newcastle United** become only the second team to win the English FA Cup on successive years by beating **Arsenal** 1–0 in extra time. They were lucky to do so since Arsenal, playing with only ten men after losing **Wally Barnes** due

Newcastle United with the FA Cup

to injury in the beginning, came near to winning ten minutes from full time when the ball ran along the Newcastle crossbar.

The English Amateur Cup went to **Walthamstow Avenue** who beat **Leyton** 2–1 in extra time, before a crowd of 100 000; and **Hungary** beat **Yugoslavia** 2–0 in the final at the Olympic Games.

Rugby Union

The year was dominated by the achievements of three teams. The **South Africans** won 30 out of 31 matches in their tour of Britain (losing only to Home Counties by 9–11) and went home with 562 points against 167. **Wales** took the Triple Crown with 42 against 14 points but lost 6–3 to **South Africa**, and the **Fijians** in a tour of Australia made a colossal impression with their attacking play and beat Australia in one game while losing the other.

Rugby League

Workington win the Rugby League Cup

A touring **New Zealand** team in England fared rather badly and was defeated in all three Test Matches. While **Wigan** dominated the Northern League, **Workington Town** beat **Featherstone** 18–10 in the Challenge Cup final at Wembley before 73 000 people.

American Football (grid-iron)

On the grid-iron

Though bedevilled by 'fixing' (see also Basketball above) the game continued at a high rate of popularity with the traditional contests in full swing. **Clarence Munn** (Michigan State) was selected as Coach of the Year and the Lambert Memorial Trophy went to **Syracuse University**. **Detroit** won the professional National Football League and **Michigan State** was unofficially rated by the Press poll as the US College Champions.

Golf

For **Britain** the major event of the year was the unexpected triumph of her women in winning the Curtis Cup against the USA,—the first time ever—by one match. Nothing so remarkable attended the men's fortunes in the international game, the British Open Championship going for the third time in four years to **A D Locke** (South Africa), the Amateur to **E H Ward** (USA) while the bulk of the men's prizes dropped neatly into the bags of US players, no one player dominating, apart from Locke. This was the year in which the stymie was abolished, the one in which **William Nary** (USA) took only 60 to do a round during the El Paso Open and

Bobby Locke

Eddie Arcaro

J Boros (USA), the US Open Champion, topped the list of Official PGA money winners with $37 032. It was also a year when players in ever increasing numbers on more and more courses topped, sliced, pulled the ball more times than ever before.

Horse Racing

The Arlington Classic, richest of the world's races ($150 450 and won by **Mark-ye-Well**) was just one among many of the top races (including the Kentucky Derby) won by the leading American jockey, **Eddie Arcaro**, who went on to become the first jockey to ride winners worth more than $2 million in one year. In June, Arcaro had become the first American-born jockey to ride 3000 winners, which was still well below **Gordon Richards** in Britain who, up to the end of September, had won 4594. In Britain Richards, with 231 winners, was Champion jockey for the 25th time in 27 years (though still without a Derby winner to his credit to the amazed disgust of the punters) and the **Aga Khan** once more won the Derby (5th time) and the St Leger, this time with **Tulyar** and **Charlie Smirke** in the saddle, to become top owner of the year with his trainer, **Marcus Marsh**, top of the trainer's table. On grass, on 18 October, **Wilwyn** (ridden by **Eddie Mercer** (Britain)) won **the first international race at Laurel Park, Washington, USA.**

Over the sticks, French bred horses did best at Cheltenham taking the Gold Cup (**Miss Dorothy Paget's Mont Tremblant**) and the Champion Hurdle (**M Kingsley's Sir Ken**). But the Grand National went to a hunter from the Scottish borders, **Harry Lane's Teal** ridden by **A P Thompson**.

Prince Ali Khan leads in Tulyar

Ice Hockey and Skating

Canada won the Ice Hockey Gold Medal at the Winter Olympic Games, beating the USA, and in so doing merely emphasised what everybody knew, that these two countries remained supreme in this sport. On the other hand, the **Detroit Red Wings** not only won the National League but took the Stanley Cup with eight straight play-offs, the first team ever to do so. **Gordie Howe** of Detroit won the Hart Trophy as most valuable

Dick Button

player as well as the Ross trophy for being the leading goal scorer in the National Hockey League.

In the Olympic Games, too, the USA produced the dominant figure, that of **Richard Button**, who won the figure skating title, having taken the national and world championships as well. Among the women, however, the top figure skating honours were distributed with **Tenley Albright** (USA) taking the US Nationals, **Jacqueline du Bief** (France) the World Championship and **Jeanette Altwegg** (Britain) the European and Olympic titles. For Norway **Hjalmar Andersen** was supreme as world Champion in speed skating and in winning Olympic Golds for the 1500, 5000 and 10 000 metres events.

Rowing

For once in a long while, the annual Boat Race between Oxford and Cambridge was a memorable event. Not only was it rowed in a blizzard but it was also a neck and neck struggle from beginning to end with **Oxford** getting home by a canvas—their first win since 1946.

At the Olympics the rowing honours were shared by **Russia, Argentina, the USA, France, Yugoslavia** and **Czechoslovakia**. The Varsity Eights Race of the USA was won by **Yale** in quite a tight finish from **Harvard** by 3.8 seconds, though the time taken, 22 minutes, 49 seconds, was the slowest since 1924. The Diamond sculls at the Henley Regatta went to **M T Wood** (Australia).

Swimming

No doubt due to the conditions, it was nevertheless remarkable that, although every Olympic swimming event except for the men's 100 metres free-style, and the women's 100 metres free-style and 100 metres backstroke, were Olympic records, not one world record was broken at the Games. Although the **USA** did best in this sport, with eight victories out of the 16 events, **Hungary** did well to take the men's polo and three women's events, while the **Japanese**, appearing for the first time since the war, took a number of Silver and Bronze medals. The **Australians**, on the other hand, had a somewhat disappointing time with only a single Gold Medal (for the men's 200 metres breast stroke) a fact that was all the more remarkable when it is recalled

Oxford on the right

Kathleen Mayoh

that their **John Marshall** recently held no less than eight world's swimming records dating from 1950 and 1951. Elsewhere, however, US swimmers captured no less than six world records.

The English Channel was swum only seven times, of which one crossing was by a British woman, **Kathleen Mayoh**. Of the men, **Victor Birkett** (Britain) made the best time in 15 hours 36 minutes. In the USA **Florence Chadwick** who, in 1951, had become the first woman to swim the Channel both ways, swam the 21 miles of difficult water from Catalina Island to the California Coast in 13 hours 47 minutes 32.6 seconds, just 12 minutes longer than the record then held by a man.

Lawn Tennis

Left to right: *Louise Brough, Maureen Connolly and the Duchess of Kent at Wimbledon*

Frank Sedgman and Jaroslav Drobny

For the third year running, and for the tenth time, Australia won the **Davis Cup** defeating the USA 4–1 and demonstrating their absolute superiority in the men's game. Earlier the women of the USA had annihilated Britain 7–0 in the Wightman Cup at Wimbledon. **Maureen Connolly** (USA) dominated the women's game (despite the presence of America's **Doris Hart, Louise Brough, Shirley Fry, Pat Todd** and players of that calibre) to win both the US and British Championships. Likewise **Frank Sedgman** (Australia) was top among the men by taking the US and British Championships, though failing at home where **Ken McGregor** (Australia) was the winner. **Jaroslav Drobny** (Egypt) won the French singles.

Table Tennis

The World Championships held at Bombay in February were notable for the first ever appearance of the **Japanese** and a display of their mastery of the game which won them four out of seven titles. **H Sato** (Japan) won the men's singles, but **Angelica Rozeanu** (Romania) took the women's singles for the third successive time and demonstrated a superiority which was to last well into the future. While this was the first year of Japanese pre-eminence (their women took the Marcel Corbillon Cup for the first of what, so far, has been eight occasions) it was the final year of **Hungarian** dominance, their last of eleven successive victories in the Swaythling Cup when they defeated **Britain** by only 5–4.

Angelica Rozeanu

Yachting

Uffa Fox, the Duke of Edinburgh and Coweslip

For the first time since 1935 Royalty took part in the Cowes Regatta, the **Duke of Edinburgh** sailing his Flying Fifteen *Coweslip* in to a second place and his Dragon *Bluebottle* in to a third place. Almost as much comment could be heard about the boats' names as the skill of the royal helmsman in what was, by the number of entries, a record year.

Ann Davison with Felicity Ann

An outstanding helmsman by the name of **Paul Elvstrom** (Denmark) won the Finn class at the Olympic Games, making it the second successive Gold in his collection, having taken the Firefly class in 1948, and just one more towards the eight world titles he was to win during his career. Two other Olympic Golds were won by the USA, one by Norway and another by Italy.

The most important race of the year, that from Newport RI to Bermuda for the Bermuda Cup, was won by **R S Nye** in the 46 ft yawl *Carina* in the corrected time of 3 days 16 hours 51 minutes, the fifth in order of placing being the British 24 ft *Samuel Pepys* (**Erroll Bruce**)

which then put back to sea to win the Bermuda to Plymouth race in 17 days 5 hours 3 minutes. In Portugal the World Star Class Championship was won by *Merope* (Italy) with 142 points.

Of the long distance voyages in progress or undertaken in 1952 none lasted longer than that of **Ann Davison**, who set out in her 23 ft *Felicity Ann* from Plymouth, England, on 18 May to eventually arrive at Miami on 13 August 1953, (the first by a woman solo across the Atlantic). She was on passage between Las Palmas and Barbados on New Year's Eve, 1953.

SECTION 7

FASHION AND DRESS

Since changes in Fashion are directly geared to the promotion of clothing sales and closely related to advertising and business, they are quite frequently exaggerated both in their original form and in their presentation. Although people can become enthused over fashion, it is more to the point that their choice of wear is governed by wealth and the necessity to dress for the everyday occasion. Therefore they seek utilitarian clothing. This was certainly the case with most of the British and many Europeans in 1952, for although the days of clothes rationing were, for the most part, over, the inflation and rising costs of 1951 had imposed a sharp fall in demand. People were hunting for bargains and, perhaps from a carry over of the habit of rationing, were content to make do with small wardrobes. So it was depressing to trade when the impetus imparted by women's fashion by fashion's self-appointed leaders was also uninspiring. Women's styles could at best be rated vague in 1952 though, by unusual contrast, the men were almost—by their proclivities—spectacular in appearance.

In Britain, the wartime **Utility Scheme was abandoned in March and replaced by the D Scheme,** which was merely a somewhat fairer way of relating Purchase Tax to textiles, while removing price controls on all shoes and clothing with the exception, that is, of nylon stockings, which were still a little difficult to come by. When demand for textiles continued to fall the Government stepped in with defence orders for clothing and by cutting the rates of Purchase Tax on clothing in May to help the failing industry. Towards the end of the year things had picked up again, and by November all the existing controls on materials had been removed. Leather prices drifted and there was uncertainty after the big 1951 up-swing. In the USA, where clothing had zoomed from 187 to 204 on the Consumer Retail Price Index in 1951, they slipped back some 4 points.

*Pierre Balman's
Crinoline Creation*

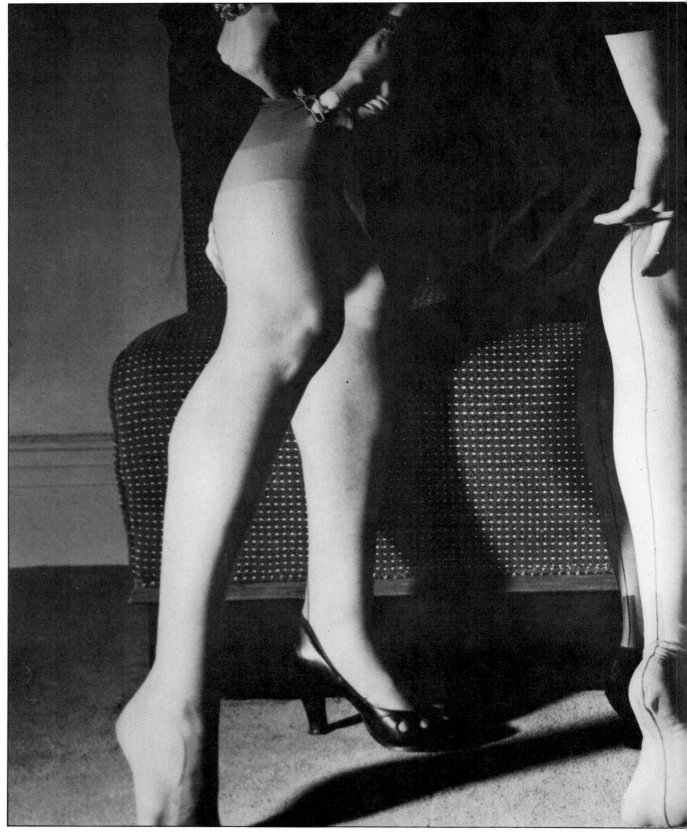

Nylons: Barbara, Australian, (right) was adjudged to have the most beautiful legs and for the record the measurements were length 32 inches, calf 13 inches and ankle 7¾ inches

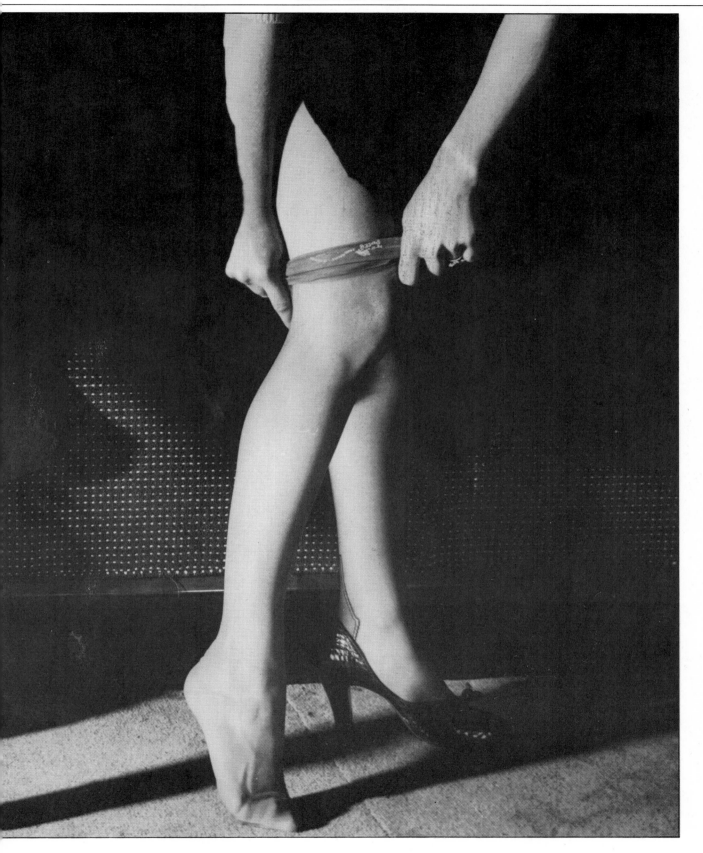

Fashion did little to stimulate enthusiasm among women; the excitement which had followed the famous Christian Dior New Look in 1947, with its 'feminine' reaction to wartime uniform, had faded and been replaced by a 'wait and see' attitude which reflected the prevalent uncertainty about how prices would move. The established women's fashion houses fell prey to indecision, as exemplified by their vacillation over the location of the waist—or whether, indeed, there should be a waist at all! In a year that lacked a grand motif, 'the wandering waistline' was the neatest epithet the critics could concoct. And the corsettiers had their flexibility stretched to the utmost in their endeavours to cope with the fluctuation of different designers' diverse demands. The hem-line settled down at the 'regulation' length of $11\frac{1}{2}$ inches from the ground (for those who really cared), and some dresses and coats were clutched tight about the body while others flowed free with wide, even, billowing skirts. It was all very confusing since, in those days, fashion trends were followed far more slavishly by the deeply fashion-conscious elite.

Price 59½ Guineas

A Dior creation

Foundations in New York!

In London a new designer, **John Cavanagh**, made his appearance, and in Paris a name which was to become established among the most distinguished couturiers arrived—that of **Hubert de Givenchy**—though neither made a revolutionary impact even though their success was immediate.

Stylists, with whom business was booming, suggested that hair ought to be permanently waved and worn short by the most fashion-conscious woman, presumably to suit the tight little 'bathing cap' hats which Paris prescribed. However, 'picture hats' were still to be seen at the great 'Fashion Gatherings' such as Ascot. Shoes, too, tended towards attenuation with heels at a moderate height and a general air of lightness, notably with those styles in which only very thin straps were used as uppers, imparting a sandal effect. No one striking

colour dominated or made its debut, a failure in originality which may have taken its tone from the basic colour of the year, which reverted to an almost wartime camouflage look of battleship grey. As in so many other things, women chose the colours that suited them personally and did not suffer dictation from the strict discipline that some connoisseurs suggested they should accept.

Choice of materials was, of course, fundamental. Furs were still in demand for coats and stoles, the ecological lobby being hardly as yet a force in deterring the killing of wild animals for this purpose. In Britain the principal deterrent to the purchase of fur, by everybody but the most affluent, was a Purchase Tax imposition of 100%. Traditionally natural materials, with a few minor innovations, continued to dominate—leather for shoes, wool

and cotton for clothing. A typical innovation for example was a fur felt material called **Melusine** that was used for hats. Increasingly the artificial fabrics, of which nylon (first commercially introduced in the USA in 1940) was predominant, were supplanting the established materials. This revolution had been delayed everywhere by the war and it was not until 1952, for example, that the **first Terylene began to appear in British shops**.

Jewellery remained, as ever, the principal decorative accessory adopted by women, with diamonds as the most popular gem stone, not only because of its attractive look but also because of its everlasting quality. Furthermore, a genuine diamond was more easily recognised and the chance of fraud minimised for the less well informed, whereas anybody venturing to invest in emeralds could so easily be tricked. For, from America, **synthetic emeralds** of close similarity to the real stone (made by a secret process originated in 1946) were beginning to appear on the market in great quantity. They were of such quality in 1952 that only comprehensive scientific analysis could isolate the true from the false. Synthetic stones such as these were expensive to produce (a figure of £20 per carat was suggested) but even so were cheaper than the real thing. Only later was it discovered that the synthetic gem fluoresces red under ultra-violet light whereas the genuine article does not.

One new gem stone was discovered in 1952 among many new minerals isolated by modern scientific methods. This was the **Sinhalite** from Ceylon which previously had been considered as yellow or brown peridot but now was recognised as a mineral in its own right. Discoveries such as these were opportune since a scarcity in coloured gems was beginning to make itself felt and prices were rising—an escalation which, in Britain, was made all the more exorbitant by the imposition of the same 100% Purchase Tax which also affected furs. Hence, in Britain, there came at this time a strong impetus in the creation of cheap costume jewellery, at its best of intricate and delicate design and employing semi-precious stones. Some were selected patriotically as emblems of their country's origin.

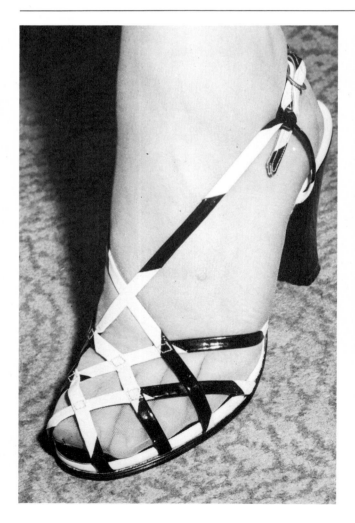

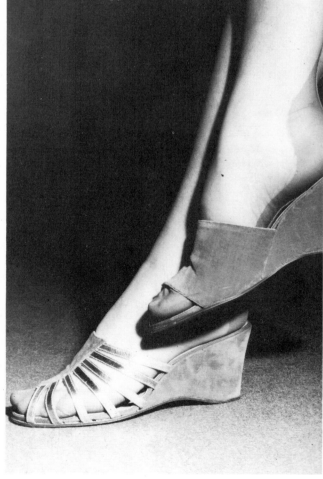

Men's fashion, by way of comparison in sartorial effect, actually began to outshine that of women. All of a sudden they began to shake off dull camouflage and to dress in brighter colours, beginning with non-matching and sometimes garish waistcoats, topping off with brighter shirts and ties and rounding off the effect with socks of a more lurid hue. In fact, colour was but one of the distinctive changes adopted by men. Shape, too, was altering since more informal occasions were attended with a slacker style and fit. The double-breasted suit, however, still had preference of choice for everyday use—the jacket received slight accentuation by long collars and lapels, and the trousers narrowed, without turn-ups. This, too, was the beginning of a neo-Edwardian period in style, the **Duke of Edinburgh** taking what was, for him, an unusual lead in matters of fashion by turning out one day in a Norfolk jacket with plus-fours.

The average men and women in the street were rarely immediately affected by the leaders of fashion. They bought their clothes from the chain stores and lesser boutiques whose products were converted from the previous years' fashions into models which could be

	£	s	d	
Women				
Brassière		16	11	(85p)
Pants		12	0	(60p)
One-piece dress	10	0	0	
Two-piece suit	20	0	0	
Shoes	2	10	0	(£2.50p)
Men				
Shirt	1	10	0	(£1.50p)
Pants		5	0	(25p)
Three-piece suit	10	0	0	
Trousers	4	0	0	
Shoes	3	0	0	

fairly easily and, above all, reasonably cheaply, mass-produced. They paid a wide range of prices for what, on the exterior, looked like remarkable identical articles, but which varied chiefly in the quality of fabric used and the standard of workmanship involved. Prices in Britain were those shown in the table above.

Women paid as much as 2s 6d (12½p) to have a single nylon stocking repaired, so precious and difficult to replace were these alluring and fragile articles of hosiery.

SECTION 8
CRIME AND CALAMITIES

The increase in crime which dated from, and was attributed to, the Second World War persisted in nearly all countries with the notable exception of Switzerland. The pattern of its growth in Europe, was regular in that many crimes which had once been rated as patriotic when committed against the occupying German forces during the war were multiplied in peacetime. Crimes of violence, on the other hand, were only marginally on the increase compared with 1951, though still very high compared with 1945; in Britain, for example, crimes such as these were up about 1 % on 1951, sexual offences 5 % and robbery (which had fallen by 23 % in 1951 compared with 1950) was also up. In the USA an appreciable increase on all crime in 1951 was extended, with the excep-

Aftermath of prison riot in a New Jersey State prison in sympathy with riots at Trenton prison on the 21 April

The shattered Redfield safe

tion of rape, and projected into 1952: there, murder was up by 3.5%, assault by nearly 10% and juvenile crime markedly higher. It was calculated that, throughout the USA, there was one larceny every 26 seconds, a rape every half hour and a murder, manslaughter, rape or attempt to kill every 4.6 minutes. Unhappily there was not one country in which the rate of prosecution kept pace with criminal offences.

Among the more notorious crimes of 1952 were:

. . . the robbery of the home of **Laverne Redfield** in Reno, Nevada, in which $1.5 million in cash, securities, and jewellery were taken. Reckoned as the USA's biggest robbery to date, it might have been worse: a suitcase containing another $1 million in securities was overlooked by the thieves.

. . . the conviction in April of a number of people connected with the vice of 'fixing' inter-collegiate sports, notably basketball in the USA (see also Section 6.)

. . . the mass escape by 300 of the 400 prisoners in the Brazilian prison on Anchieta Island in June, when 17

people were killed. Most of those who got out were quickly rounded up.

. . . the case of **John Straffen** in Britain, who had been convicted in 1951 of strangling two children, found insane and sent to Broadmoor asylum. Escaping from there in May, he killed another child before recapture, but this time was sentenced to death because, though mentally defective, he was declared not insane. The trial was of unusual interest since evidence was admitted in connection with the previous murders. On appeal, Straffen was reprieved and returned to an asylum.

. . . the murder in August of **Sir Jack Drummond**, (a noted British dietician), his wife and child while they were camping in France. Though the identity of the culprits was in some doubt in 1952, enquiries by the French authorities pointed in the direction of the Dominici family, whose farm lay a short distance from the scene of the crime. A holding charge was laid against **Gustave Dominici**, whose evidence was conflicting.

. . . the gang-land type murder in the USA in March, of **Arnold Schuster**, after he had given information which led to the arrest of **William (The Actor) Sutton**, a much wanted bank robber.

John Straffen

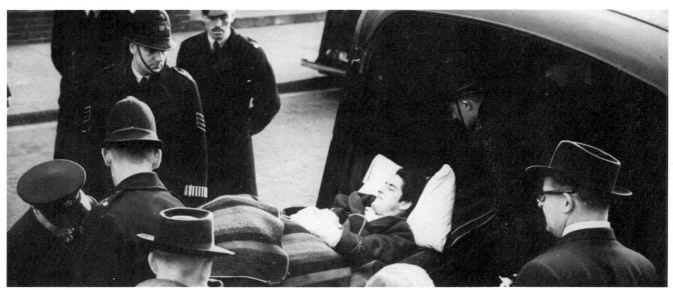

Christopher Craig

... the murder in November of a British policeman **Sidney Miles** by the 16 year old **Christopher Craig** after a roof-top chase in Croydon.

... the murder in London by **Dennis Muldowney** of the Polish **Countess Skarbeck** who, before the war, had been a 'Miss Poland' and during the war, as **Christine Granville**, one of the most successful and brave operatives working behind the German lines in Europe. Four times decorated, she had consistently avoided capture (except once when she talked her way out of arrest by the Gestapo) while accomplishing many outstanding exploits with sang-froid and ruthlessness.

In East Germany, in October, measures were introduced with the intention of making crime a more forbidding venture. The prosecution was given almost unlimited powers; theft of state property, or even its contemplation, were made punishable by forced labour; police evidence was made almost sacred and the independence of judges nullified. There were those who asked if this Act of State was not one of the more serious crimes of the year, a calamity of the era, though there were others in the West who might have subscribed to the beliefs of the **Archbishop of Seville** when he called freedom of thought, of religion and the press 'liberties of perdition'.

For those who suffer from a set-back or a death in the family it is no recompense if the event happened to occur as part of a celebrated calamity. For individuals the impact of a deep loss is personally shattering, whatever the circumstances, though easily made all the more painful should the occasion, through some sensationally unusual aspect, become common knowledge through wide publicity. Sensational tragedies, of which there are relatively few out of millions each year, can set the tone for the period of the nine day wonder because they are bizarre, gigantic or in some way remarkably coincidental in their relation to other disasters. A recurrent type of crash may lead to speculation as to sabotage or some weird, unheard of defect in human behaviour or in machinery—or it may miss the news reports altogether. Awesome natural and uncontrollable calamities, such as earthquakes, exert a morbid attraction special to their inevitability and are assured of wide publicity.

Calamities got off to a quick start on 3 January with an **earthquake** of minor dimensions in a part of the world accustomed to such terrors. A shock centred on **Hasan-kale** near Erzurum in Eastern Turkey, affected an area that included 17 villages. Considerable damage was done, 62 people were killed and 250 injured, while many more were made homeless. This was the usual pattern, but here the plight of the survivors was made worse due to severe frost and heavy snow which prevented relief operations getting quickly into their stride in what was, at the best of times, difficult terrain.

A type of disaster, so familiar that sometimes they receive only local mention, occurred at the **McGregor coal mine** at **Stellaton**, Nova Scotia, Canada on 14 January when an explosion killed 19 men underground. The pithead, as is tragically normal on these occasions, was the scene of a vigil by fearful relatives, as rescue parties quickly got the survivors out and recovered the dead.

Since **air crashes** were an almost daily occurrence only the dramatic, the poignant or those with a high casualty list received prominent news coverage. Among the poignant kind, with a high casualty roll, was the DC 4 which crashed into the water near **Sandspit Airport**, British Columbia, on its way back from the Far East, with US Army veterans returning from the war in Korea; 36 out of 43 on board were killed. However, the crashes which hit the headlines hardest were those in built-up areas and, in particular, a succession of three in the vicinity of **Newark Airport**, New Jersey, USA.

The first, on 16 December 1951, had involved a C 46 of Miami Airlines with engine failure due to faulty maintenance which plunged into the Elizabeth River, killing all 56 aboard. This was the **second worst accident**

Aftermath of the crash at Elizabeth on 22 January

in US aviation history at that time. On 22 January an American Airlines Convair, flying off course in bad weather, swerved on approach to the runway and struck houses in **Elizabeth**, killing seven of the dwellers besides the 23 passengers in the aeroplane, one of whom was Robert Patterson, a former Secretary for War. From the same runway a National Airlines DC 6 suffered from a reversed propellor on take-off and hit a 50 apartment house in Elizabeth killing four residents and 29 flyers. Although there was no kind of relationship between each crash, except that the runway happened to be the same on each occasion, the resultant outcry was sufficient to have the airport closed for an inquiry, as it remained until 16 April when it was reopened for military use. In the meantime the public's anxiety had led to widespread investigations into air operations close to cities. There was a demand for tightening up of all procedures besides the installation of better navigation and safety equipment, a programme which received further impetus on 5 April when a US Airlines C 46, making its approach to **Idlewild** (today's Kennedy Airport), fell into the residential area of **Jamaica**, killing two of the crew and two civilians. Newark was reopened to airlines, subject to limited use, on 16 June after an inquiry by **General James Doolittle** had said in May that it was safe. Doolittle did not wholly agree with **Eddie Rickenbacker**, the president of Eastern Airlines, when in February the latter claimed that Newark was the 'best situated, the best equipped and the safest in the entire country'. Full operations were not resumed until November, when a new $10 million runway came into operation.

Those at Newark were the more eye-catching, sensational crashes. In January, alone, there were twelve major accidents involving many deaths and in February a further eight, one of which involved a US B 29 heavy bomber on 7 February near **Tokyo**, killing its crew of 13 along with five Japanese. And on 22 February, near **Pusan** in Korea, a fighter aircraft hit a power station, a hospital and four houses to kill 15 and injure another 20.

February was a month of extremely heavy snowfall in Europe from which came a harvest of calamities caused by **avalanches**, or through people being cut off and dying from exposure. Skiing parties were frequently in peril. In all 75 people were to die from snow and ice in Austria that month, the worst episode taking place on the 10th when 19 Germans were buried after an avalanche struck and demolished an inn near **Mittelberg**. Hardly a day passed but somebody was caught by one of these horrifying catastrophies, which could kill by the atmospheric pressure of air on the lungs raised by the snow's passing.

The worst earthquake of the year had its centre 45 miles out to sea off the island of **Hokkaido**, Japan. The first main shock came at 10.24 am on 4 March and was to be followed by eleven minor shocks; some felt in Tokyo, 420 miles away. Waves 6 to 8 ft high were raised and swept ashore, swamping fishing boats and dashing among the coastal towns. At **Shiranuka** 1000 houses were destroyed and over 10 000 people left homeless. Fires broke out, two trains were derailed and there was panic in **Kushira**. Nevertheless casualties, at 29 dead and 159 injured, were remarkably light, partly due to adequate warning having been given, and largely because the area affected was relatively lightly populated.

On the same day **the worst train accident of the year** occurred. A heavily overloaded train on its way to Rio de Janeiro was crossing a bridge over the River Pavuna, when a broken track derailed two cars. Soon after an electric train was involved in a head-on collision leaving 119 dead and 250 injured. In this instance signalling faults were the cause. It is a commentary on the way news was distributed that, strangely, this crash was not reported in *The Times* of London.

That scourge of the USA—**the tornado**—manifested one of its more hideous outrages on 21 March. Raging down the Mississippi valley it vented most spite on **Judsonia**, Arkansas, where about 200 died and the town was devastated. It also swept through south-east Missouri, northern Mississippi, western Kentucky and

Alabama smashing property, bringing fire and, along with heavy rain, floods to cause damage amounting to a sum that was rated at several million dollars. It further took a toll of lives that eventually reached 236, with 2500 injured. At once the Army and emergency services moved in and the Red Cross allocated $1 million for relief and earmarked a further $4 million if required. The Reconstruction Finance Organisation (RFS) declared the affected zone a 'disaster area' and announced it had $80 million available for loans.

Within a matter of days, however, a still greater threat appeared to the northward as the winter snows began rapidly to melt and send a tumult of water pouring down the **Missouri River** to recreate a nightmare situation which had previously occurred but a year before. **Flooding** began in Montana and the Dakotas on 6 April and spread remorselessly downstream to inundate 123 cities and close 45 railroads and 115 highways, rendering 100 000 people homeless and causing immense losses to stored crops and other property, which was eventually to be estimated at costing $300 million. Thousands of people turned out to work alongside Army Engineers in strengthening the levees, but 325 of these barriers broke before the force of water. For three weeks danger was

present, often contained, sometimes too strong for men. Loss of life seems to have been low since there was ample warning, but politics were immediately to the fore, invoked by President Truman who took the opportunity to tour the worst hit areas. He described the floods as the

Tornado damage in Ohio

The Missouri floods

worst he had ever seen and claimed that if Congress had not blocked his earlier proposals for dams the disaster could have been avoided. In the aftermath, Truman proposed to Congress a $1.5 billion plan to insure people and organisations against flood losses, besides restoration of the original flood control plans he had submitted. From this came, at last, in years to come, the ambitious **Missouri River Basin Program** (or Pick-Sloan Program as it was then known) that was to lead to an alleviation of flooding in the future besides the development of a healthy commercial river traffic.

In the meantime August 1952 produced the cynical paradox of a drought so severe in many of the previously flooded zones that, again, they were proclaimed disaster areas.

A disaster without physical cause, but which came about through human frailty, overwhelmed the good sense of the congregation of **Santa Teresa Church in Caracas** on 9 April. A false fire alarm turned people from worship to the primitive urge of self-preservation. For ten minutes a scrum of desperate men, women and children fought to leave the building, crushing under foot the weak, the infirm and the unlucky. When the building was empty 53 bodies lay among the many injured. Easter services in other parts of the city were cancelled.

Three amateur mushroom growers of Tottori caused the greatest Japanese fire of the year when, on 18 April, they decided, illegally and most unwisely, to tap a main power line to use the electricity in their hut. Fire started in the hut and spread to engulf 5000 houses (about 40% of the town) and cause damage amounting to about $41 million. The mushroom growers survived and were charged with their crime.

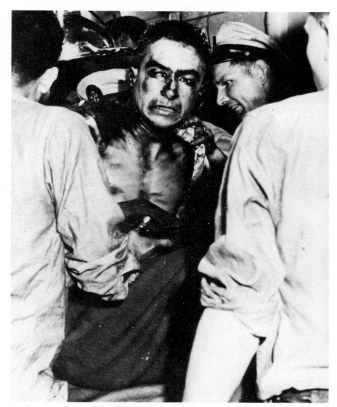

A Survivor of the USS Hobson

USS Wasp *after the collision*

The biggest loss of life in a single incident during 1952 came about while the US aircraft carrier *Wasp* was engaged on 26 April upon night manoeuvres in the Atlantic. As close escort she had two destroyers, one of which was the 1620 ton destroyer *Hobson* (converted for minesweeping). In good weather conditions, *Wasp* gave warning that she was about to take on aircraft and began to turn into wind at a speed of about 25 knots. Errors on the part of the commander of *Hobson*, however, placed

her on a collision course and the *Wasp* ripped open the destroyer which sank very quickly. Out of the crew of 223, 176 were lost, among whom was the commander of *Hobson*, who subsequently was found responsible for the accident.

It had been a bad period for the Armed Services of the USA. In February the extensive Army/Air Force winter exercise (with atomic strikes simulated) which had been based on Camp Drum had ended with 'victory' for the defenders, the imagined casualties on the two sides being

Earthquake damage at Bakersfield, California

extensive. The real ones were also high—9 dead and 170 injured from a succession of accidents. And on 21 April the cruiser *Paul*, operating off Korea, received damage that caused 30 deaths.

The typhoon season got off to a rather early start by bursting upon the Philippines on 2 July with winds of up to 155 mph that caused 10 000 people to become homeless and killed 85. However, this was the gentlest of prologues to what was to happen later in the year in the same region and elsewhere in the Far East.

The ever worrying dread of earthquakes with which the citizens of California live was stimulated once more on

when the aircraft broke up. Fuselage, wings and one engine crashed onto the airfield, killing the crew, while one of the engines curved away to the left and plunged among the crowd, where it was thickest at the best vantage point, killing 28 spectators and injuring another 63. After the roar of the jet there came an awesome silence, but there was no panic as rescuers came forward. A few minutes later the show went on as **Neville Duke** took the Hawker Hunter aloft and coolly delivered another sonic boom straight at the crowd. The next day people were once more watching the show seated on the site where the engine had fallen.

The exact moment of impact of the DH110's engine into the crowd at Farnborough

21 July by a severe shock centred upon **Tehachapi**. Out of a population of 2000, 14 died amid scenes of considerable disruption; the shock was widespread and felt from **San Francisco** to **San Diego** and in **Phoenix**, Arizona. A great fire started in an oil refinery 14 miles from **Bakersfield**, a woman's prison was so damaged that the inmates had to be housed in a tented camp, while a railway train narrowly missed calamity when a tunnel, through which it had just passed, collapsed. A month later there was another shock, this time in Bakersfield itself, where two died, 32 were injured and $20 million of damage was caused.

The fall of 9 inches of rain on Exmoor on 15/16 August which caused the River Lyn to change course and pour through the town of Lynmouth, Devon, was rated the **worst English natural disaster of the century**. It killed 31 people, did £2 million of damage, and so ravaged the town that it had to be evacuated for a fortnight while public services were restored and repairs made to the centre of the town. (See Section 1 for further details).

At the Farnborough Air Show on 6 September, a DH 110 twin-engined fighter, flown by **John Derry**, with **Anthony Richards** as observor, had just completed a dive from 40 000 ft to break the sound barrier and send the familiar triple boom over the enthralled crowd, and was returning to make a 500 mph pass across the airfield,

Spraying locusts in Jordan

In April warning signs of a **locust invasion** were found in Jordan, one of the traditional breeding grounds. Counter measures by spraying and burning began and it was announced that it was not thought to be a serious threat. However, as the summer advanced so, too, did the locust swarms flying into India and Pakistan and descending upon an area estimated at 8000 square miles, in numbers that could add up to a weight of 500 tons per acre, each insect capable of consuming ten times its own weight in green vegetation. This was an unusually heavy migration which, fortunately, could be mitigated by the use of the latest insecticides (aldrin in particular) which were frequently sprayed from light aircraft. Yet many found their way as far east as Assam, and Delhi too was threatened. To nations that were already short of food, this was a dismal business.

The French submarine *La Sibylle* (previously the British *Sportsman*) put to sea with a crew of 48 on 24 September for diving exercises off St Tropez in the Mediterranean. After that nothing more was heard of her. A search soon revealed a large oil slick 6 miles east of Cape Camarat, and the submarine's rescue buoy was also picked up in water that was between 380 and 440 ft deep. It could only be assumed that she had got out of control and broken up.

On 8 October, the Perth to Euston express was so delayed by fog and diversions that it was running 90

Above: La Sibylle

Below: *Wreckage at Harrow and Wealdstone*

The platform at Harrow and Wealdstone station

minutes late. At last, in patchy fog, the highly experienced driver was just getting into his stride, working up to 50–55 mph as he approached **Harrow and Wealdstone Station** at the height of the morning rush hour. Standing in the station was a commutor train picking up passengers. For some unknown reason the driver of the express ran through a 'distant' signal set at caution and two 'stop' signals set at danger without in any way slowing down. Only at the last moment did he see the danger, by which time he was about to hit the back of the stationary train with an impact like a bomb exploding, hurling debris all over the platform. Worse was to follow as the dust began to settle. The Euston to Manchester express, coming from the opposite direction, was already past the last 'stop' signal and thundering amid the chaos to multiply the carnage. A scene of utter devastation awaited rescuers and first aid workers. Eventually 112 dead and over 200 injured were found from the three trains and those on the platform. In the aftermath official attention was drawn to tardiness over the years in fitting semi-automatic signal warning devices, such as had been in operation on the Western Region since early in the century. Rather feeble excuses of a bureaucratic technical nature were offered in reply, but there was an ostentatious flurry of progress after this crash, though an automatic traffic control system for British Railways non-electric trains was still not approved by the Ministry of Transport until four years later.

Typhoons struck with full force along their normal routes at the end of October. **Indo-China received the worst buffetting in its recorded history** at a time when the

devastating war which was to last 30 years, reached a new peak of violence and intensity. While French and Viet Minh troops grappled in the jungle and among the villages, full force winds ripped through **Siam** and **Cambodia** and then hit **Saigon** before ravaging on to the **Philippines**. A total of 300 died in Indo-China, 444 in the Philippines in addition to 2000 said to be missing. In the Philippines the town of **Legaspi** was ruined and total damage costs amounted to $50 million. It was **Formosa's** turn on 14 November, when another typhoon hit the south-western part of the island killing 67, injuring more than 500 (including many soldiers in a barracks) and doing extensive damage to crops including a large part of the banana harvest.

Just before Christmas, on 22 December, two major tragedies spoiled the festive season. In **Vorarlberg**, Austria, an avalanche thought to contain 200 000 tons of snow, threw a bus off the road and killed 23 of the passengers, most of whom probably dying from the effect of atmospheric pressure on their lungs; 19 of the dead were British, the others French. And in Japan, after fire had broken out in amonium sulphate at a **Nagoya factory**, there was an explosion in a hydrogen tank which made a crater 25 ft deep and 30 ft across, killing 30 people and injuring 500 more.

Commenting upon the apparently large number of **air crashes** that came to his notice, a British coroner asked if there was not something remarkable about the number of men being killed in jet aircraft? He was referring probably in the main to pilots under training; and, of course, an air crash through its dramatic impact usually received panic attention in the newspapers. It is noteworthy that, whereas the enormous number of accidents in the home or on the roads were mainly lumped together as part of the annual statistical summaries, air accidents tended to receive individual treatment. So it is possible to extract the number of *reported* dead which, from one review, came to 1237 though undoubtedly this was incomplete, particularly since many military incidents were played down and accidents in the Soviet Union and among its satellites only rarely achieved publicity. Yet it is worth remembering that in the USA at that time it was estimated that, while there was a fatal accident of some sort every 6 minutes, road deaths were the biggest killers at one every 14 minutes. . .

Above: *Typical road crash*

Below: *Fire in the home*

SECTION 9
OBITUARIES

Among the distinguished people who died in 1952 were:

Sir Montague Burton (b 1885): his name was prominently displayed to the British public on the distinctive facades of the large tailors' shops which sold the cheap mass-produced clothing for which he was famous. Burton was a self-made man who began work as a tailor's assistant and opened his first shop in 1900 on £100 capital. At his death there were many shops backed by a large manufacturing concern run on progressive lines, whose workers were well cared for. Much of his wealth was spent on philanthropic projects, above all on the support of higher education, art and literature.

Sir Stafford Cripps (b 1889): his last job in the British Labour Government had been as Chancellor of the Exchequer (1947–50). Cripps was the proponent of a strictly controlled economy which came to be known as 'Austerity'—which, to the day of his death, was associated with British economic policy, even under the Conservatives. A member of the Labour 'left' he had first entered Parliament in 1929 when his reputation as a lawyer was already well established. Made Solicitor General in 1931, he soon relinquished office due to disagreements with Labour Party policy and he was expelled from it in 1939. In 1940, however, Churchill sent him to Moscow as Ambassador. From that moment his ascent to high office was assured, despite his many critical pronouncements on the conduct of the war. In missions to India in 1942 and 1946 his attempts to resolve the problem of devolution of power were unsuccessful, while his spell as Chancellor was in part notorious and epoch-making because of the radical devaluation of the pound in 1949 from $4.03 to $2.80.

John Dewey (b 1859): the US philosopher whose principal contribution was in the field of education by applied psychology. He travelled widely giving advice and was internationally famous. His progressive approach, which was practical and experimental and centred upon the child rather than the subject, drew sharp criticism but, nevertheless, imposed a strong formative influence on US educational policy which is still felt 25 years later.

Sir Patrick Hastings (b 1880): a British lawyer and the Attorney-General in the first Labour Government (1924) whose (suggested) part in withholding evidence in the case against the editor of the Communist *Workers' Weekly* led to the Government's fall that year. Though fairly successful as a playwrite and author it was for his forensic skill, particularly his tussles with **Norman Birkett** in criminal cases, for which he was best remembered.

Aleksandra Kollontai (b 1872): the first Russian woman Cabinet Minister of the Communist regime. In 1923 she gave up a post in the Commissariat of Foreign Affairs to become Minister for Norway, the first of several similar appointments to Mexico and Sweden, where she was Ambassador in 1943, just prior to negotiating the end of the Soviet–Finnish War in 1944.

Sir Stafford Cripps

Sir Patrick Hastings

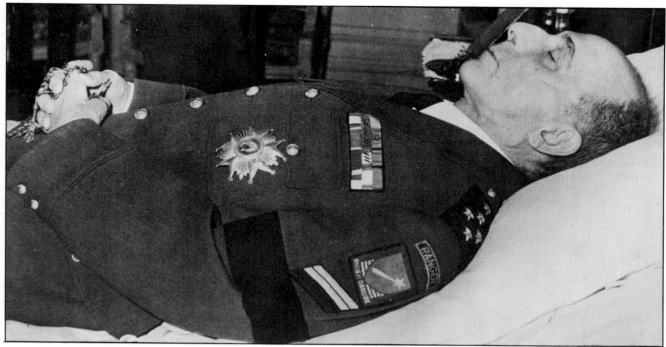

General de Lattre de Tassigny

General Jean-Joseph-Marie-Gabriel de Lattre de Tassigny (b 1889): France's last great Marshal (posthumously created). He was among the handful of French generals to command with distinction in the debacle of 1940 and, as commander of the French First Army, led the advance from the South of France in 1944 to the German frontier. After a spell as C-in-C Land Forces, Western Union, he was sent to Indo-China in 1950 where, in less than a year, he brought hope out of despondency among the hard pressed French in their long fight against the Viet Minh. The final collapse of his health came when the impact of his efforts were being demonstrated in battle.

Gertrude Lawrence (b 1898): the beautiful actress, singer and dancer whose greatest successes were won in revue during the 1920s and subsequently in the 1930s in **Noel Coward** plays, notably *Private Lives*. Her last role, at the time of her death, was as Anna in *The King and I* on Broadway.

Viscount Linlithgow (b 1887): who had been Viceroy of India from 1936–43 and therefore responsible for the initial abortive attempts to arrange a devolution of British power in India. India's declaration of war on Britain's side in 1939 made by Linlithgow, without consulting Congress, undermined his authority. The rest of his time in office was spent in creating a strong war effort, despite the internal conflict stirred up by the civil disobedience campaigns of **Mahatma Ghandi** and his followers.

Maria Montessori (b 1870): Italy's first woman to win a medical degree, was most renowned as one of the great

Gertrude Lawrence

Maria Montessori

educational reformers. It was she who encouraged mentally deficient adults and children to read and write by the use of teaching aids and by mobility in the classroom. A brilliant lecturer, she spread her ideas worldwide in prolonged tours and by writing.

Eva Peron (b 1919): the small-time Argentinian film-star who married **Juan Peron** in 1945, just in time to help him, by her charm and vivacity in his campaign, to win the Presidential election. Once in power he made her Director of the Social Aid Foundation with authority over Health and Labour. Immensely popular with the workers, upon whom she lavished benefits, she won privileges for the poor and for women, while antagonising the middle classes and the rich. Her attempt to become Vice-President in 1951 was prevented by the Army at a time when her health was already failing.

Eva Peron

Elizabeth Schumann (b 1888): the great German *Lieder* singer and creator of the role of Sophie in Richard Strauss's *Der Rosenkavalier*. Of world wide renown and possessor of a soprano voice with special qualities which emerge even from the oldest of her gramophone records, she departed her native land when the Nazis occupied Austria, disgusted with the turn of events. A supreme interpreter of Richard Strauss, she was also outstanding in her performances of music by Beethoven, Mozart and Wagner.

Elizabeth Schumann

Chaim Weizmann (b 1874): a Russian Jew and an excellent biochemist, who came to head the Zionist organisation in 1918 in Palestine and spent most of the rest of his life leading those who aimed at creating a Jewish national homeland. In 1948 he became provisional president of the newly created state of Israel and the next year, after the first Arab invasion had been defeated, its first President.

Chaim Weizmann